THE COMPLETE GUIDE TO
BIRD
DOG
TRAINING

THE COMPLETE GUIDE TO

BIRD
DOG
TRAINING

JOHN R. FALK

Revised Edition

THE LYONS PRESS
Guilford, Connecticut
An imprint of The Globe Pequot

Copyright © 1976, 1986 by John R. Falk

First Lyons Press paperback edition, 2006

The Lyons Press is an imprint of The Globe Pequot Press.

10 9 8 7 6 5 4 3 2 1

Printed in the United States of America

ISBN-13: 978-1-59228-855-7
ISBN 10: 1-59228-855-3

The Library of Congress has previously cataloged an earlier (hardcover) edition as follows:

Falk, John R.
    The complete guide to bird dog training / John R. Falk.-
Rev. ed.
      p. cm.
    Includes bibliographical references and index.
    ISBN 1-55821-319-8
    1. Bird dogs-Training. I. Title. II. Title: Bird dog training.
SF428.5.F34   1994
636.7'0886-dc20   94-10124
                                                  CIP

DEDICATION

To all the ''girls'' in my life,
both two-footed and four-footed,
this book is affectionately dedicated.

CONTENTS

PREFACE

Winning a million dollar sweepstakes is a pleasure very few of us ever are likely to enjoy. Most average folks must be content with the innumerable small pleasures life doles out. Certainly, to a hunter, one of the best of these is the opportunity to gun over a good bird dog, properly trained to perform eagerly, happily, and in a manner both pleasing to the eye and productive for the game bag.

There are four ways to avail yourself of this opportunity: (1) Hunt with a friend who owns such a dog; (2) Buy a mature dog, already fully trained; (3) Buy a puppy and eventually have it trained by a professional; (4) Buy a puppy and train it yourself.

Although option number one is by far the least expensive and carries no personal responsibilities, it is also less gratifying than the other three. Option number two begins to become more personal, but means you'll miss about two of the most interesting years of the dog's life. The number-three choice enables you to enjoy the early frolics of a fantastically ingenuous, lovable young pup, before having to turn him over to a professional trainer for several months annually, at least for a couple of years. Finally, there's alternative number four, which is really what this book is all about.

Naturally, not everyone who attempts to train a bird dog will be successful. Persons of certain temperaments seldom attain good results. The lazy, the indecisive, the timid, the inconsistent, the overly brusque, or the too busy owner ordinarily produces bird dogs that accurately reflect the tenor of the training they've received.

Yet, assuming you're of stable character, have a genuine desire to tackle the job, can devote reasonable time and effort to it, and have access to some open land, you should have no hesitancy about being able to turn out at least a serviceable bird dog, and at best, perhaps, a highly polished one. How far you go toward either goal will be mostly up to you, and the kind of bird dog pup you choose.

Helping you to set up your own guidelines by which to determine not only the type of dog—pointing or flushing—but the breed that's most suitable for you is one of this book's primary aims. What should prove to be a deeply gratifying personal experience can well become a bitterly frustrating disappointment if you start off with the wrong kind of dog.

Preface

What to do after you acquire the right kind of puppy to transform it into an efficient bird dog is, of course, the book's main objective. The training methods suggested are proven ones; they will, if properly applied, produce successful results with a majority of canine pupils. But, should you run into the exception, don't be discouraged. Do some research, read a number of other bird-dog training books, and then think out your problem. Be innovative, if necessary. Above all, don't be hasty or impatient. The dog you train today will provide you with years of service, devotion, and companionship.

John R. Falk
South Salem, N.Y.

THE COMPLETE GUIDE TO
BIRD
DOG
TRAINING

CHAPTER 1

WHICH BREED FOR YOU?

Training a bird dog involves a good deal of commitment, responsibility, and decision-making. In fact, to make the project a success, decisions will become a daily necessity in your bird-dog training routine. The most basic and important decision is choosing the right *type* and *breed* of bird dog to train for the hunting you want to do now, as well as for the next ten to twelve years. (If you already own a bird dog puppy, you can only hope it was the right choice. If it wasn't, you may still be able to rectify your error by giving the puppy away or swapping it for another more suitable breed.)

In deciding which bird dog breed to buy, you'll probably be motivated by such unscientific considerations as gut feelings, eye appeal, popularity trends, childhood reminiscences, snobbery or—worse yet—what the neighbors might think. All these reasons will guarantee you a poor, if not disastrous, choice.

For instance, if you were to choose an Irish setter puppy solely on the basis that you've always thought the red setter is the most beautiful dog in the world, chances are you'd be making a great mistake in your selection of a suitable bird dog. If, however, you were to choose the Irish setter after learning something about the breed—its temperament, size, disposition towards training, average mental and physical development, hunting technique, etc.—and then applying

1

Which Breed For You?

Opposite:
For many people the English springer spaniel, a flushing breed, makes an ideal choice for field and home. His medium size and affectionate disposition make him adaptable to small quarters and young children. He is the nemesis of all ring-necked pheasants. Photo by Robert Elman, courtesy of Leonard Lee Rue III.

Below:
The two most traditional pointing breeds in North America are the English pointer (atop stone fence) and English setter (below). Both are used to hunt major upland-game birds, but the pointer generally is better adapted to warm-weather hunting while the setter excels in cooler climates. Photo courtesy of Gaines Dog Research Center.

that knowledge to what you know about yourself—your own temperament, personal circumstances, life-style, game-bird preferences (realistically tempered, of course, by their availability in your own hunting territory)—the odds would be heavily in favor of your having made a good or even perfect choice.

Actually, there is really only one practical way to choose the most suitable type and breed of bird dog, and that is to start from scratch, discarding all preconceived preferences and extraneous considerations. Once you clear your mind and adopt a systematic approach, choosing the right bird dog breed becomes relatively easy. (Detailed descriptions of the qualities, characteristics, and talents of ten of the pointing and flushing breeds we personally recommend will be found in Chapters 2 and 3.)

Since your initial concern involves what your dog will be expected to do in the field, the following points must be considered: (1) The principal upland game birds in your area; (2) Of the upland game birds available, the one or two species you most enjoy hunting; (3) The average temperature range encountered in the vicinity you will be hunting during the open season for birds; and (4) The physical characteristics of the terrain and cover you'll be hunting most of the time.

By jotting down your responses to these points, you'll find that you have all you need to begin zeroing in on the type and breed of bird dog you should consider owning. For example: (1) if the principal upland game birds in your area are ring-necked pheasants, ruffed grouse, and woodcock; (2) if you enjoy hunting pheasants and woodcock more than ruffed grouse; (3) if the average temperature range encountered is about 35 to 45 degrees; (4) if the terrain in which you'll be hunting consists mostly of open fields and brush lots, in gently rolling hill country—then with a little research you'll discover that all of the breeds recommended in Chapters 2 and 3 could certainly be used to hunt both ring-necks and woodcock. However, it will also become apparent as you read about them that the breeds used as flushing dogs—such as the springer spaniel, the Labrador and golden retrievers, and the American water spaniel—are far better bets than any of the pointing breeds when it comes to hunting pheasants *most* successfully. The fact that the flushing types do not equal the pointing breeds for sheer thrills and pleasure on woodcock need not bother you too much since woodcock would only be an occasional target for you anyway.

By now you have probably figured out, assuming the circumstances outlined above apply to you, that the type of dog you need is a flusher, rather than a pointer, and that, if you stick to the suggested list, you can narrow your choice to four different breeds. You also know, from your own observations and the breed descriptions, that any one of these four can physically withstand both the climate and terrain, as well as the kind of cover predominating in your hunting grounds.

That's fine, as far as it goes, but now you have to determine how to select the best breed out of these four candidates. And that's where the following questions can assist you:

1. Will your bird dog live indoors with you and your family?

2. How is your home best described—roomy, small, or downright crowded?

3. If your wife will bear most of the responsibility for the daily care, feeding, and walking of the dog, is she willing and able to handle a large, medium, or smallish dog?

4. Are your children (if any) old enough to cope with learning to live with a bird dog who'll share their home with them?

5. How would you describe your own temperament—easy going and patient; strict and strong-willed; calm and perservering; nervous and easily excitable?

6. Of the breeds available, which one really appeals to you most?

Obviously, the answers to these questions cannot be quite as cut-
' dried as the ones that led you to select the type of bird dog (flushing or pointing) best suited strictly to your field-hunting needs. In order to see how these questions might be applied, let's take a hypothetical hunter and see how he handles them. By so doing, we will give you an example of the kind of dialogue you might engage in with yourself in choosing your dog.

Question #1: Yes, I plan to keep my bird dog indoors with me and my family.

Question #2: We live in a rather small house, five rooms in all; not really spacious—well, in fact, rather cramped.

Question #3: I'll have to rely on my wife to care for the dog during the week, but she knows this and is willing. Since she's only 5'2" and about 108 pounds, I guess a medium or smallish dog would be easiest for her to handle.

Question #4: We have two children, a boy, nine, and a girl, four. The boy is typically active, likes and relates well to animals, but ducks long-term responsibilities for them. The girl is shy and very sensitive, loves pets, and is usually gentle with them.

Question #5: In all honesty I regard myself as a calm, patient person, by nature perservering but seldom intolerant.

5

Question #6: Instinctively, my first preference among the breeds recommended would be the Labrador retriever, but the springer spaniel is a close runner-up.

The size of the breed, of course, is of utmost consideration, especially if the dog will be living indoors with the family in a compact and crowded home. For example, the Labrador retriever may have to be ruled out of consideration in the case of our hypothetical hunter simply by virtue of his size; he could prove to be too much dog for a small house. On the other hand, the springer spaniel is of much more compatible size under some circumstances. And, although somewhat soft by nature, the springer would pose no problem getting along with the youngsters, or for that matter with anyone who is patient and unexcitable.

There are, however, two other breeds among the flushing dogs recommended in Chapter 3 to be checked out before a final decision is made. The golden retriever, like the Labrador, might have to be eliminated from contention strictly on the basis of size. Not so the American water spaniel, though. A bit smaller than the springer in size, he is small enough to coexist in a small, rather crowded home environment. And, again like the springer, his slightly sensitive disposition would match up ideally with the temperaments of our hypothetical family. In terms of his abilities as a pheasant hunter, he'd have to be classified as a good, serviceable worker, although, on average, a notch or two below the springer.

So, having double checked all the candidates on the author's suggested list, our hypothetical hunter may conclude that he should be able to choose the springer spaniel, satisfied that the breed meets all his major prerequisites both for home and field. But it's still not time to rush right out to buy one; it may not be exactly the right breed for him.

Only you can provide the accurate personal information needed to assess each breed and the merits and disadvantages it offers within the limits of your own individual circumstances. The most important

---

Above:
Although a bit too large for cramped homes, the Labrador retriever has an ingratiating personality and makes a good flushing dog in the uplands.

Below:
A trio of vizsla pups appears very much at home in an easy chair. The vizsla is one of the world's oldest pointing breeds. Photo courtesy of Marion I. Coffman, Cariad Kennels, Weston, Conn.

thing to remember, as you go about formulating your answers to the key questions, is the need to be candid and objective. If you fudge even the least bit, you'll be defeating the whole purpose of your analysis and may wind up with a breed you won't be happy owning.

If your responses are honest and complete, you may even find that the logical choice of breeds indicated by your answers will be at odds with your own personal preferences. If such proves to be the case, you'll have no alternative but to compromise somewhere. How? Well, suppose, for example, our hunter concluded that he simply

---

Opposite:
Among the first considerations you'll have in choosing the right type and breed of bird dog are the principal upland birds available in your area. Here a gunner begins swinging on a fast-crossing cock pheasant.

Below:
The only member of the spaniel family that points rather than flushes his birds is the Brittany spaniel. This one, Dual Ch. Gringo de Britt, combines high-headed pointing style with excellent conformation. Photo courtesy of American Brittany Club.

couldn't live without a Labrador retriever. Since the breed's size could create an impossible hardship living indoors with the family, his only resort would be to keep him outdoors all year in a backyard kennel—a workable alternative, but, nevertheless, a major compromise.

It's possible, too, that you may not find a breed that seems precisely right for you among the six pointers and four flushing dogs recommended in Chapters 2 and 3. Although compiled on the basis of personal opinions, experience, and judgment (further details of which are explained in the next chapter), the list is only a partial roster of the sporting dogs recognized by the American Kennel Club that have been used at one time or another to hunt game birds in North America. The complete roster, numbering twenty-four, would include among the pointers, the German wirehaired pointer, the Irish and Gordon setters, and the weimaraner; among the spaniels, the clumber, the American and English cockers, the field spaniel, the Irish and American water spaniels, and the Sussex and Welsh springer spaniels; and among the retrievers, the Chesapeake Bay, and the curly-coated and flat-coated retrievers.

Thus, if you honestly can't pinpoint what you believe to be the right breed from the ten suggestions, your alternative will be to start researching some, or all, of the other breeds that make up the complete sporting dog roster. The suggested reading list included in this book should prove helpful to you in locating further information on these additional sporting dogs.

CHAPTER 2

SIX POINTING BREED CANDIDATES

If there are twenty-four different breeds of sporting dogs eligible for registration in the American Kennel Club, you may wonder why only ten are recommended as prime candidates for your consideration. Is there something wrong with the other fourteen? Aren't they good gun dogs? Or is the writer simply pushing all of his own favorite breeds?

To the last question, we can say with absolute candor, no! Certainly, among the ten breeds we've selected are some of our favorites, but they are not included merely on that basis.

Neither do we mean to imply that the fourteen breeds omitted are not good gun dogs. Some of them have been scratched primarily because of their extreme rarity in North America. Others have been excluded because one or more breeds on our recommended list are very similar though, in our personal opinion, a bit more consistently desirable. Still others have been deleted for exhibiting what we believe to be deficiencies in performance, potential, or personality.

The recommended breeds have been picked because they encompass the widest scope of possible considerations pertinent to a majority of upland bird hunters in North America today. Collectively, this group of ten offers virtually every significant qualification any American or Canadian bird hunter could reasonably ask for or require.

So, let's take a close look at each of our prime candidates, starting with six of the breeds that point their birds for the gun.

THE ENGLISH SETTER

Whenever pointing dogs become the topic of conversation among serious upland bird hunters, two breeds are certain to be focused upon as the benchmark of style, class, and hunting intensity against which all others pale by comparison. This duo is the English pointer (more often referred to nowadays simply as the pointer) and the English setter. Both are as traditionally well ensconced in North America as popcorn and apple pie, and have been padding around the bird coverts of our continent longer than any other pointing breeds.

For sheer good looks combined with gentle temperament, companionable nature, and spirited hunting desire, the English setter is considered by many to be unrivalled among all the breeds that point birds for the gun. Strong natural pointing instinct, sensitive scenting powers, and a good memory for lessons learned through training and on-the-job experience are qualities that help explain why the breed has withstood so well the test of time as a favorite American pointing dog.

The setter's primary job afield is to search for and find game birds, then pinpoint their location for the gunner by "freezing" in a statuesque pointing stance. He tackles his work diligently, casting about the cover and thoroughly investigating the birdy spots out front. Constantly quaffing the air currents, he'll pick up the faintest aerial scent given off by his feathered quarry, follow it to its source, and then stand stiffly on point until the hunter arrives to flush and shoot the bird or birds. If he's a natural retriever—and a fair percentage of setters are—or has been force-trained to retrieve, he'll

---

Above:
For sheer good looks combined with gentle temperament, companionable nature, and spirited hunting desire, the English setter is regarded by many as top dog among all the breeds that point birds for the gun.
Below:
The setter's longhaired coat gives him ample protection against thorny, brush-filled covers and serves equally well in insulating him from cold weather.

fetch the downed bird gently to hand after the hunter's successful shot.

The setter's long-haired coat of soft, almost silky texture provides him the protection he needs against the brushy tangles and thorn-filled covers he is often called upon to hunt. His coat serves equally well for insulation against the cold weather so frequently encountered in the northern half of the continent, where he enjoys his greatest popularity. His predominantly white coloration makes him easily visible both in motion and on point, even in the densest thickets.

Although some canine historians believe the English setter's origin stemmed from a combination of crossbreeding the Spanish pointer, the large water spaniel, and the springer spaniel about two centuries ago, other students of the breed contend that the English setter is really more than 400 years old. The latter argue that the setter was a natural outgrowth of the land spaniels, which were in use in Europe during the last several decades of the fourteenth century.

In his treatise, *Le Livre de la Chasse* (*The Book of the Hunt*), written in 1387, Gaston de Foix, a nobleman who spent most of his spare time hunting, spoke glowingly of the land spaniels and also mentioned a distinct kind of "setting" spaniel. Almost 200 years later, Dr. John Caius, in his book, *Of Englishe Dogges,* graphically described the performance of the "setting" spaniels, leaving no doubt that they halted in their tracks and put belly to earth, thus indicating the presence and location of game over which the hunters spread or threw nets to entrap it.

This "setting" tendency—really a modified form of what later came to be known as pointing—was obviously deemed desirable by some hunters of that day. In order to preserve and intensify the trait, they selectively bred only those dogs that displayed it most strongly to others imbued with the same characteristic. Soon, the specialized spaniels that "set" themselves for the net throwers acquired the

---

Above:
Warm, affectionate, and appealing are terms commonly used by those who know the English setter intimately. Here, Shoshone Ghost Dancer waits patiently in his station-wagon crate for his master to take him bird hunting.

Below:
Almost any English setter from field-proven ancestry should have all the right instincts, in varying but generally sufficient degree, to become a productive bird dog when properly trained.

nickname "setters," a designation that finally became the official surname for three separate and distinct pointing breeds: the Irish, Gordon, and English setters.

By the time firearms eventually displaced the hunter's nets for the taking of upland game birds, the "setting" position that required the dogs to "point" with belly touching the ground underwent a logical transition, changing from prone to a modified crouching stance.

Although the early "setting" spaniels were to be found in various parts of Europe, it was in the British Isles where the setter's major development occurred. From a single pair of reportedly "pure" English setters, Edward Laverack, a well-to-do Englishman who began a serious breeding program in 1825, bred a strain that took his name, and during the ensuing thirty-five years gained international fame as gun dogs.

In the mid-1860s, a Welshman named R. L. Purcell Llewellin did some further building on Laverack's bloodlines, crossing them with other setters of that period to produce a strain bearing his own name. In almost no time at all, the English setters known as "Llewellin's" achieved top hunting dog status both in the British Isles and in the United States, where they were imported shortly after the Civil War.

Today, most of the English setters of hunting ancestry in North America are of the Llewellin type, while those of predominantly Laverack type now hold sway strictly as bench show competitors. Unfortunately, these show-bred setters, although beautiful, have little value as gun dogs in the field.

The modern North American field type English setter comes in a variety of sizes. The smallish ones can tip the scales at as little as 35 pounds soaking wet. The average-size setter gun dog, however, generally weighs a good 10 to 15 pounds more and stands a bit higher on leg. Mostly white—for easier location by the hunter—the setter's long-haired coat normally is ticked and/or patched with such secondary colors as black, black and tan, lemon, orange, chestnut, or russet. His legs and full-length tail carry extra-long, plumelike hair called "feathers." While his long-haired coat gives the setter excellent protection both from cold weather and punishing cover, it has the disadvantage of burring up after a hard day's work in the field. The deburring an owner must do later on might most charitably be

---

A close bond of affection is usual between the English setter and his family. At ten months of age, however, Shoshone Meridee Missi was
a bit large for her mistress's lap.

termed a labor of love. Few setter owners linger nearly as long discussing the subject as they do on the deburring act itself.

In range and pace the setter can vary quite a bit; some naturally running fast and wide, others staying in fairly close and moving at a steady trot, and still a third type fitting in roughly between these two. Topography, type of cover, and species of game birds prevailing in the area where a setter was bred and trained usually prove to be the main determinants. No matter what his natural range and pace may be, though, the well-trained setter should be expected to adjust his speed and distance from the gun, according to the dictates of the cover he's hunting at any given time. This does not mean that the really fast, big-going setter is the proper type for you if most of your gunning is limited to close cover conditions. Such a dog is not practical for use in heavy cover.

The English setter is usually thought of as a ruffed grouse and woodcock dog. Traditionally, these two game birds have provided him with the lion's share of his work. But in recent years, the setter has begun to enjoy ever-increasing favor in the southern and southwestern United States for hunting bobwhite quail. In truth, there are relatively few upland game birds the English setter cannot be trained to handle with good-to-excellent results. Any bird that will lie reasonably well to a pointing dog can be considered fair game for him.

The setter is least desirable or productive on those types of game birds that prefer running rather than sitting tight or flushing when confronting danger. Prime examples are the various desert, mountain, and valley quails generally found in the semiarid regions of North America. This is no great loss for the breed, since such areas are synonymous with hot, dry weather conditions under which setters cannot work well for sustained periods.

Almost any English setter with a good background of fieldworking ancestry can be counted upon to have all the necessary instincts to become a productive bird dog when properly trained. Extremely good-natured and very affectionate, this breed normally takes to training with enthusiasm, especially when it's given in firm but gentle fashion. Some setters require very careful handling, while others have tough hides and can stand up under fairly harsh discipline. Yet, the vast majority of setters fall in between these extremes and will respond best to a firm voice, reinforced, when necessary, with a bit of moderate physical chastisement.

A good part of the setter's appeal as a gun dog lies in his stylish way of going in the field. Working mainly on airborne body scent to locate his birds, he almost always hunts with a high head and a merry tail, displaying a graceful, rhythmically fluid motion on the run. On point he is seldom anything less than an intense, exciting sight to behold, and often is a virtual calendar picture of regal loftiness.

Yet, as handsome and efficient a field performer as he is, the English setter possesses even more potent qualities at home. His warmly affectionate nature, combined in a personality sparked with just a dash of high-spirited devilment, makes him irresistible. As a good family pet, the setter deserves the consideration of anyone whose home is roomy enough to accommodate a medium-size breed with an oversized heart full of companionship and devotion.

The breed is officially sponsored in the United States by the English Setter Association of America, a member breed club of the American Kennel Club, in which most bench show setters are registered. English setters from working field stock—the kind that hunt—are generally registered in the Field Dog Stud Book, the registry operated by the American Field Publishing Company, 542 South Dearborn Street, Chicago, IL 60605.

In typical grouse and woodcock cover the English setter's predominantly white coat makes him visible on point. Setters normally reach their peak at between four and five years of age.

SUMMARY

ENGLISH SETTER	(From working field stock.)
TYPE	Pointing breed.
WEIGHT	35 to 53 pounds (average 43 to 50 pounds).
HEIGHT AT WITHERS	21 to 25 inches.
COAT TYPE	Longhaired.
COLOR	Primary color is white; secondary color (patched and/or ticked) is black, black and tan, lemon, orange, chestnut, or russet.
TAIL	Full length and feathered.
MATURITY	18 months.
DISPOSITION	Gentle and affectionate; makes good house pet.
GAME BIRD SPECIALTIES	Woodcock, ruffed grouse, bobwhite quail, Hungarian partridge, sharptailed grouse, pinnated grouse, sage grouse. Setters can be used for ring-necked pheasants and other birds that run a lot, but results on such other birds are apt to be spotty and frustrating to dog and owner.
HUNTING RANGE	Can be found in various types—close, medium, and wide. On average, though, setters are more apt to be medium to medium-close.
TRAINABILITY RATING	Generally enthusiastic to learn and eager to please; respond best to gentle firmness. Lessons once learned are seldom forgotten.
OTHER REMARKS	Not well adapted to excessively hot weather; require water frequently while hunting; coat gathers burrs, especially in feathers on legs and tail.

THE ENGLISH POINTER

If any gun dog breed can qualify as "a veritable hunting machine," it is the English pointer. Not that there is anything "mechanical" about his work; far from it, for he displays all of the qualities most admired in the high-class pointing dog—flashy style, good speed, redoubtable range, and lots of staying power. He is simply a breed that truly loves to hunt more than anything else.

Like the setter's, the English pointer's basic job afield is the quest for game birds that he accurately locates by aerial body scent and points for the gunner. After the birds are flushed, he may be called upon to retrieve, a chore he seldom takes to naturally, but for which he usually must be "force-trained."

Particularly well suited for warm-weather hunting, by virtue of his short-haired coat, the pointer has long been the kingpin pointing breed of the southland, where he and bobwhite quail are synonymous. The bobwhite and the pointer just naturally go together.

Seventeenth century Spain is cited as the pointer's time and country of origin by some authorities. Others are not as certain of this as they are about his ancestry, supposedly an amalgam of one or more hounds, including foxhound, greyhound and bloodhound, eventually crossbred with "setting spaniels."

The pointer's principal development took place in England. Several of the noblemen who contributed so substantially to the breeding programs that enhanced the rise of the English setter also took special interest in breeding, developing, and improving the English pointer.

For a time after the first field trial ever held—in 1865, in England—pointers were not permitted to compete with setters, but had to be run in separate stakes. Reports of those days indicated the performance of the average pointer lacked any semblance of the sparkle, zest, or bird-finding ability exhibited by the setters; consequently, there existed a sort of *"nolo contendere"* status between the two breeds.

That the tide of battle turned is tribute to the breed and the stalwart faithful who brought it from obscurity to its present position as top field trial breed in both England and North America today.

The modern-day English pointer in North America owes a great debt to his field trial-oriented backers, past and present. Without the need to be extremely competitive and to meet the extra-high standards to do so, the pointer might not have developed the qualities and natural talents that make him the bird-finding hunting machine he is.

21

For the man whose all-consuming desire is an accumulation of varicolored field trial rosettes, the pointer has to be the most logical choice. But the breed can just as easily satisfy the longings of the man who dreams only of experiencing some of the classiest pointing dog work in the world, while simultaneously getting the chance to knock down half-a-dozen or so quail per outing.

Most field-bred English pointers weigh in at between 55 and 70 pounds. Males stand about 24 to 26 inches at the withers, while females are usually an inch or two shorter. The breed's short-haired coat is predominantly white, with patches and/or ticks of such secondary colors as liver, orange, lemon, or black. He sports a full-length tail, which whips back and forth gaily while he's at work in the field.

Seldom picking up burrs or other foreign matter, the pointer's short-haired coat is easy to keep well groomed. In addition, it proves to be the right length for hot weather. Conversely, though, it is not adequate protection in the often cold northern regions. Nor does it serve successfully to safeguard the dog against the skin-slashing thorns and briers of the heavy grouse and woodcock coverts of the upper half of the continent.

Essentially, his working style and game finding and handling methods are the same as the English setter's, although the pointer generally runs faster and wider than the average setter. However, there are English pointers to be found that tend toward less ranginess and slower pace. But one would have to look at many more pointers than setters to find the same number of slower, closer workers. Such types are referred to in the South as "singles" dogs, meaning that, because they are more deliberate hunters, they do better at finding the tight-lying single quail from a scattered covey, than they would at locating the bevies themselves. This latter job is the specialty of the speedy pointers that cover large gulps of territory in no time at all, making long casts to birdy objectives and not wasting efforts or energies in hunting barren areas.

Above:
Good style and intensity on point are characteristics of the typical field-bred English pointer, a breed that quests for and locates birds primarily by aerial body scent.

Below:
Most English pointers are not inclined to become natural retrievers, preferring to be off again looking for more live birds, rather than fooling around with dead ones. They can, however, be force-trained to retrieve.

23

Since a majority of pointers are best classified as "covey dogs," the man who hunts big open chunks of country will derive most benefit from the breed. As already emphasized, bobwhite quail are the pointer's specialty. But practically any of the upland birds worked successfully by setters can be handled with equal aplomb by the English pointer. He would not be especially recommended, however, for the man whose primary interest is hunting ruffed grouse, strictly because he lacks the kind of coat needed to withstand the rigors of cold and cover conditions in typical ruffed grouse country.

The pointer usually develops fairly early in the field, normally

---

Opposite:
Generally a dog of the big, open country, most English pointers are most adept at hunting covey birds, such as bobwhite quail and Hungarian partridge. Snow on the ground here belies the fact that pointers are best adapted to warm-weather hunting.
Below:
The most consistent winner in pointing dog field trials, the English pointer nevertheless can easily satisfy the man who simply wants a classy pointing dog along with the chance to put a few birds in the bag.

reaching the peak of his field performance about a year or so earlier than the English setter—that is, at about three to four years of age. And because he takes so readily to bird hunting, his schooling can be pushed a bit faster by an impatient owner than would ordinarily be advisable with most other pointing breeds.

The pointer's boldness, independence, and indomitable spirit permit the administration of fairly stern discipline without his wilting like a bruised pansy. And that is most fortunate since harsher methods often have to be applied to bring an extraordinarily eager pointer under the control required for productive gunning results.

As is true of the setter, the pointer usually displays the kind of stylish movement on the run and lofty carriage on point that most

Opposite, above:

A force-trained-to-retrieve English pointer fetches up a plump chukar partridge. The average pointer's boldness and independent nature permit him to take fairly stern discipline, something often necessary in teaching force retrieving.

Opposite, below:

With such stylish movement on the run and fiery intensity on point, it's no wonder the English pointer has so many staunch supporters.

Below:

The English pointer's mostly white, shorthaired coat seldom picks up burrs and is easy to keep well groomed.

bird hunters feel is more than half the pleasure of gunning over a dog. Many of the breed's staunchest supporters contend they'd rather shoot half a limit over a classy English pointer than a two-day limit over a more productive but far less spectacular breed.

In the home, the pointer might be characterized as a friendly boarder, rather than an overly companionable pet. Because of their independent nature, most pointers neither show nor require more than scanty affection.

Inasmuch as the pointer averages about 60 pounds, he would hardly prove to be a suitable house dog where living quarters are less than spacious. Yet, he does make an ideal kennel dog.

Since there are two distinct types of English pointer—one bred solely for the bench, and the other strictly for the field—if you're buying a pointer, be certain that you obtain one backed by several generations of working ancestry. Bench type pointers are always registered with the American Kennel Club; hunting pointers are usually signed up with the American Field Publishing Company's Field Dog Stud Book. The official sponsor of the breed in the United States is The American Pointer Club, a member club of the A.K.C.

SUMMARY

ENGLISH POINTER	(From working field stock.)
TYPE	Pointing breed.
WEIGHT	55 to 70 pounds (average 58 to 63 pounds).
HEIGHT AT WITHERS	24 to 26 inches.
COAT TYPE	Shorthaired.
COLOR	Primary color is white; secondary color (patched and/or ticked) is liver, orange, lemon, or black.
TAIL	Full length.
MATURITY	12 months.
DISPOSITION	Bold, independent, spirited; make only fair house pets, but good kennel dogs.
GAME BIRD SPECIALTIES	Bobwhite quail, Hungarian partridge, sharptailed grouse, pinnated grouse, sage grouse. Pointers can be used for ring-necked pheasants and other birds that

	run a lot, but results on such birds are apt to be spotty and frustrating to dog and owner.
HUNTING RANGE	Can be found in various types—close, medium, and wide. On average, though, the majority of pointers will run fairly fast and wide.
TRAINABILITY RATING	Extremely enthusiastic, natural bird hunters; quick to develop and to learn but need firm hand and sometimes stern discipline. Pointers generally need an annual refresher course to keep under proper control.
OTHER REMARKS	Very well adapted to hot weather; need little water while hunting; short coat requires little grooming, but does not offer proper protection in really rough cover or cold weather.

THE BRITTANY SPANIEL

One of the most popular of the hunting breeds imported to North America in relatively recent years, the Brittany spaniel has proved a formidable rival to the older and longer established English setter and pointer, and with good reason: pleasing appearance, practical hunting range and pace, and excellent house pet qualities.

Although his spaniel name belies his hunting technique (all other spaniels flush their game), the Brittany is a true "pointer." In fact, he is the only spaniel who does point, rather than dash right in and flush his game birds. Like all pointing dogs, the Brit casts back and forth ahead of the gun, testing the wind for bird scent, which he'll follow like steel to a magnet until he halts in his tracks, indicating the game's whereabouts. Following the flush and killing shot, when he gets the command to fetch, he'll gather in the fallen quarry and deliver it tenderly to his master's hand.

A long-haired, soft-textured coat enables the Brit to fend off the rigors of rough brambly cover, as well as the often stinging chill of fall in the northern climes. Chiefly white and patched with orange or liver colors, his highly visible coat is a distinct advantage in the shadowy stands of pine or the sun-dappled alders, where grouse and 29 woodcock like to hang out. Its major disadvantage, however, like that of the English setter's, is its affinity for gathering burrs.

The Brittany spaniel has a long history of use in Europe. Some cynologists speculate that the breed's earliest roots go back to the fifth century A.D., the time of the Irish invasion of Gaul. Dogs brought along by the invading armies from Ireland, so the story goes, were abandoned for various reasons and eventually bred to the dogs

Opposite, above:

Unlike other spaniels, the Brittany spaniel is a true pointer. This one, My Sunny Boy, owned by Bob Unger, Middleburg Heights, Ohio, displays lofty carriage on point. Photo by Conrad Jocke, courtesy of American Brittany Club.

Opposite, below:

A brace of Brits demonstrates how it's done, with F. Ch. Rufus Rastus Johnson Brown (left) pointing while F. Ch. Way Kan Fritts honors. Photo courtesy of American Brittany Club.

Below:

Intelligent and affectionate, the Brittany spaniel has become one of the most popular pointing breeds in North America. Ch. Panamuck of Brookside, owned by Tom Fisher, Portland, Ore., is seen here in fine head study. Photo by John Sapp, courtesy of American Brittany Club.

native to France at the time. Supposedly, therefore, the Irish dogs contributed to the ancient bloodlines from which the Brittany spaniel sprang.

In any event, the Brittany took many forms through the centuries and was held in great esteem by the citizenry of the French province for which the breed is officially named. The peasants used Brits to hunt a wide variety of game including rabbits, hares, and the large European woodcock.

The first of the Brit's ancestors to which the present-day breed's most unique physical peculiarity is attributable were whelped over a century ago in Pontou, a tiny hamlet in Brittany. There, from the mating of a white and mahogany-colored bitch, belonging to a local hunter, and a lemon and white dog, owned by a visiting British sportsman, the first two tailless Brittany spaniels were produced. Although just one survived to breeding age, his hunting talents along with his ability to reproduce litters of tailless and/or stub-tailed puppies made him a popular stud.

The Brittany's modern history began shortly after the turn of the twentieth century. A French sportsman, Arthur Enaud, undertook to improve the Brittany spaniel breed, which was showing definite signs of degeneration, because of too much inbreeding. Enaud's work with the breed was marred only by his lack of complete or detailed record-keeping. He is known to have utilized several different crosses in achieving his aims, which included restoration of the old Brittany's white and orange coloration, and intensification of the breed's pointing instinct and scenting ability.

It is believed that Enaud crossed into the Brit several Braques (a type of pointing dog of that day) as well as the Irish setter and the English pointer. In any case, he succeeded in freshening and invigorating the Brittany spaniel and starting the breed on the road toward the fine bird dog it is today.

Above:
His typically spaniel nature makes the Brittany eager to please, but he cannot be handled brusquely. This pup, named Dr. Buckley, is owned by Alice P. Lynch, Ridgefield, Conn. Photo by George N. Schatzel, D.V.M.
Below:
Best described as handy sized, the average field-bred Brittany spaniel weighs about 34 to 40 pounds. These Brittany pups have a ways to go to reach that size, but they already have their share of winsome personality. Photo by Jerome Knap.

The first known pair of Brittanys was imported to the United States in 1912. No others followed until the early 1930s, and it took another twenty years for the breed to catch the public's fancy. Today, the Brit, as a gun dog, is among the top four pointing breeds in North America. Contributing to this strong standing is his handy size: the average field-bred Brit tips the scale at between 35 and 40 pounds, and stands from 17½ to 20½ inches at the withers. This means the breed is easy to transport, kennel, house, and care for.

In range and pace, the Brit is pretty close to being what a majority of upland bird hunters consider ideal. Most Brits are medium-close, lively hunters, possessed with a pleasantly animated working style. As with many pointing breeds, it is possible to find some individuals that have been developed to range wide and fast. Such dogs are usually representative of the strains produced primarily for major circuit field-trial competition.

It is also possible to find Brits that range so close and hunt so deliberately that they truly earn the derogatory tag of "grass-

Although some Brits are born tailless, most have stub tails like this one. Tailless or not, a well-trained Brittany spaniel, one that will point solidly and retrieve to hand, is an extremely practical bird dog.

34

A top-notch house pet, the average Brit is gentle even with little tykes and small enough to adapt well to modest quarters. Photo by C. J. Hibbert, courtesy of American Brittany Club.

prowling shoe polishers'' usually hung on them. But for the most part, the Brit hunts enthusiastically and far enough from the gun to be considered a very practical pointing dog.

Obviously, nose, or scenting ability, is one of the hunting dog's most important assets, and nose is something the Brit has plenty of. To go along with it, he suffers no lack of determination, a formidable combination in hunting any kind of upland bird. Capable of working virtually any of the more common game birds, the Brittany is ordinarily categorized as a grouse and woodcock dog. Certainly, there is little room for argument concerning his specialization on both of these fine game birds. Yet, increasingly, the Brit seems to be making fair numbers of converts among western hunters who chase up and   35 down country fit only for mountain goats in search of chukar partridges.

There is really no good reason why the Brit should perform so well on these semiarid area birds, except for the fact that his work in such terrain keeps him basically within gun range, and the chukars he bumps accidentally rather than points on purpose are shootable. Thus, this makes him a pretty good dog for the job, especially for those hunters who aren't as fussy about good pointing dog form as they are about putting birds in the game pocket.

Usable on ring-necked pheasants, the Brittany fares as well on the big birds as do any of the close to medium-close working pointing breeds. Although he experiences the same basic difficulties any pointer has with birds inclined to run out from under a solid point, many of the ones that flush wild in front of him are very often within gun range. Thus, the productive end results justify the means in the minds of a great many pheasant hunters.

However, the best trained Brittany is a joy to behold on any bird that lies well to a point. And, although not ordinarily rangy enough to qualify as a big-country bobwhite quail dog, the Brit has practical usage for hunting the smaller fields and woodlot edges around them for pint-sized bevies that have survived in areas shrunken by rapidly encroaching civilization.

His typical spaniel nature makes him a fairly eager retriever, once he knows that retrieving is fun for him and that it pleases you. Yet, because of that same spaniel disposition, the Brit cannot be handled brusquely. Like most spaniels, he is exceptionally fond of his owner and family, and, while not as openly demonstrative as a springer, he offers and expects to receive reasonable amounts of affection.

Treat the Brit roughly and he'll become sulky and introverted; but cajole him with a gently persuasive hand, rebuking him vocally far more often than physically, and he'll usually respond well to training for home and field.

As mentioned earlier, the Brittany is a top-notch house pet, gentle enough to get on well even with young children and small enough in size to adapt to modest quarters. The fact that he is either tailless or stub-tailed has some very obvious advantages where house and car doors, as well as heavy-footed humans, are concerned.

The breed is officially sponsored in the United States by the American Brittany Club, a member breed club of the American Kennel Club. Most Brittany spaniels are registered with the A.K.C.; many are also registered with the American Field Publishing Company's Field Dog Stud Book.

SUMMARY

BRITTANY SPANIEL	(From working field stock.)
TYPE	Pointing breed.
WEIGHT	30 to 40 pounds (average 35 pounds).
HEIGHT AT WITHERS	17½ to 20½ inches.
COAT TYPE	Longhaired.
COLOR	Primary color is white; secondary color (patched and lightly ticked) is orange or liver.
TAIL	Either tailless or 4-inch stub.
MATURITY	14 months.
DISPOSITION	Gentle and affectionate, though not too demonstrative; makes good house pet.
GAME BIRD SPECIALTIES	Woodcock, ruffed grouse, chukar partridge, sage grouse, ring-necked pheasants. Can also be used for hunting bobwhite quail in small, pocket covers.
HUNTING RANGE	Can be found in various types—ultra-close, close, medium-close, and medium-wide. On average, though, Brits are apt to be medium-close.
TRAINABILITY RATING	Ordinarily eager to learn, he develops early if properly encouraged; but can be sulky if pushed too gruffly. Usually needs gentle persuasion and only mild punishment.
OTHER REMARKS	Takes naturally to retrieving; has strong pointing instinct; is handy-sized; smallest of all pointing breeds; coat gathers burrs.

THE GERMAN SHORTHAIRED POINTER

What the English pointer is to the serious field trialer, the German shorthaired pointer is to the man who only feels comfortable afield with the weight of something more substantial than a pair of sandwiches in his game pocket after a morning's hunt.

37

No, we're not intimating that the man who owns a shorthair is automatically a game hog. What we are saying is that the shorthair is "a good provider," and the man who is more interested in solid results than in spectacular style is seldom unhappy with this breed.

The German shorthaired pointer is employed in the field for the same job that all pointing dogs do; he simply goes about it somewhat differently. Yet, like the others, he quarters the ground ahead of the gun seeking hot bird scent and, once zeroing in on his feathered objective, assumes the rigid stance known as the point. After the hunter has put the quarry to wing and then permanently back to earth once more, the shorthair, upon command, will retrieve it promptly and efficiently.

Unlike the English setter, English pointer, or Brittany spaniel, however, the German shorthair spends a good deal of his time seeking and following foot scent, rather than relying mostly on body scent, to find and nail down his birds. With his head down and nose to the ground so much, he does not exhibit the attractive agility or graceful hunting style so admired in the breeds that ply the breezes with heads held high.

Doubtless the shorthair's ground-trailing proclivities trace back to the hound blood infusion believed to be part of the breed's early ancestry. Reputedly, the breed had its inception in Germany roughly three centuries ago. Canine researchers concur that the Spanish pointer, a basic hunting breed that had overspread the European continent during the early part of the seventeenth century, was among the original forebears of the German pointer. There is

---

Above:
The German shorthaired pointer will please the hunter who's more interested in putting birds in his game pocket than in spectacular style. Here, however, style and intensity on point are exhibited by C. Adam von Fuehrerheim, owned by Robert H. McKowen, Leacock, Pa.

Center:
Like most of the versatile hunting dogs, the German shorthaired pointer has a deeply ingrained affinity for retrieving. This seven-week-old shorthair pup eagerly fetches a pheasant wing. Photo by Robert H. McKowen.

Below:
More open-coated German shorthairs, such as the eight-week-old pup, are seen today than in former years. Large-framed, darker-colored dogs were more typical of earlier imports. Photo by Robert H. McKowen.

considerable conjecture, however, about whether the bloodhound or the old St. Hubert hound was crossed into the Spanish pointer to create the German pointer.

It wasn't until the 1860s that the German breed was crossed with the English pointer, which added greater range, agility, and scenting power, plus stronger pointing instinct, to the German dogs. Later on, some setter blood may have contributed additional pointing intensity and some gentleness to what became the modern German shorthaired pointer around the turn of the twentieth century.

Originally bred and trained for utilitarian hunting purposes, the first few shorthairs imported to the United States during the mid-1920s caused little excitement. Having been used to hunt hares, varmints, and to trail wounded big game, as well as point and retrieve birds in Germany, the shorthairs initially brought here proved far too sluggish in pace and restricted in range to interest most North American bird hunters.

By meticulous selective breeding over the ensuing years, a number of changes were effected, making the breed more appealing, primarily as a bird dog. His range and speed were increased and the color of his coat lightened—three aspects that very definitely accounted for a rapid rise in his popularity rating.

Today's German shorthaired pointer is seen in two basic types: the large-framed, solidly built dog, refined from but still resembling the original imports; and the far more streamlined, if distinctly muscular dog that looks rather like an English pointer with a docked tail. This latter type ordinarily sports a coat containing a much larger percentage of white than the older types and, thus, is easier to see moving or on point.

This breed has a short coat, normally patched and heavily ticked with liver coloring, except in some of the more open-coated specimens mentioned above. Although shorthaired, the German seems better adapted to handling the punishment that heavy cover and cold northern weather can inflict than does the short-coated English pointer. But, then, the shorthair doesn't tackle a piece of cover with the same reckless abandon and speed normally shown by the English pointer. Nor is he as likely to become overheated and as susceptible to chill as the hyperactive pointer.

Despite his large size, the average German shorthair should be given family pet status, if room permits. He forms close attachments with people and makes an excellent companion and watch dog. Photo by Robert H. McKowen.

As is true with the other pointing breeds, it is possible to find big-running shorthairs, mainly from strains produced to compete in field trials with pointers and setters. However, the average shorthair hunts at relatively modest range and an easy-going pace. Among the breed's most desirable field credentials are a good nose and tenacious determination to find game. Toss in the kind of stamina needed for an all-day hunt, plus a deeply ingrained affinity for fetching dead or wounded birds, and it becomes increasingly clear why the shorthair pleases so many sportsmen today.

Opposite, above:
Most shorthairs require a firm, no-nonsense approach to training. They respond best to a masterful, decisive form of schooling. This young shorthair "Whoas" on owner's hand signal and voice command. Photo by Robert H. McKowen.

Opposite, below:
With a ring-neck rooster nicely pinned in a cornshock, this German shorthair displays good style on point as his owner walks in to flush and shoot. Photo by Robert H. McKowen.

Below:
If kept kenneled right from the start, a German shorthaired pointer pup can be conditioned to outside quarters. These six-week-olds are about weaned and ready to find new owners. Photo by Robert H. McKowen.

For essentially the same reasons that enable the Brittany spaniel to hunt the ring-necked pheasant with fair success, the shorthair, too, can be regarded as a pretty good pheasant dog, for a pointing breed. His close, deliberate hunting style puts wild-flushing birds, or those that he may accidentally bump, within reasonable gun range a good percentage of the time. And the shorthair's excellent ground-trailing abilities and thoroughness usually succeed in putting any cripples in the hunter's bag.

The German can normally be counted on to turn in a serviceable performance on almost any game bird found singly, in covers compatible with his moderate range and pace. Big, open country covey birds that require a dog to cover large chunks of territory to the sides and ahead of the hunter, consequently, would have to be considered the least easily handled quarry for the average shorthair.

Most indicative of the breed's practicality—and certainly typifying the leisurely kind of hunting at which he excels—is the shorthair's place as the number one pay-as-you-go shooting preserve dog. Few pen-raised, planted birds, including pheasants, bobwhite quail, and chukar partridge, can elude him and, because once properly trained, he'll hunt and handle for anyone, he is generally considered to be the ideal breed for hunting on commercial shooting preserves.

One quality that makes the shorthair a prime candidate as a bird dog is his rugged temperament. Call it stability, or perhaps stoicism, but the average German shorthair seems to have an extraordinary ability to overcome most of the errors committed by an inexperienced heavy-handed trainer. The fact that the breed is a bit inclined toward stubbornness may create the need for tough discipline; but, at the same time, he has the ability to accept and profit from it. Most shorthairs require a firm, no nonsense approach to training and will respond best to a masterful, decisive form of schooling.

The shorthair is a big dog, most males measuring about 25 inches high at the withers and weighing up to 70 pounds. But, because he forms close bonds with his family and makes an excellent watch dog, as well as a good companion, he should be given house pet status if possible. The fact that he has a docked tail adds to his desirability in the home, since neither children nor adults are apt to tromp accidentally on a stub tail or slam a door on it.

If necessary, the shorthair can be relegated to a backyard kennel, but he cannot be considered one of the best or most mannerly kennel dogs as a rule. Most shorthairs—at least those that have had even a small taste of family life indoors—seem to defy all efforts to keep them confined, somehow finding ways to climb over, dig under, or chew through any except the heaviest chain link fence. However, if kept kenneled right from the start, a German shorthair pup can be conditioned to outside quarters without too much extra trouble.

The German shorthaired pointer, along with several other breeds—the German wirehaired pointer, the vizsla, the weimaraner, the wirehaired pointing griffon, the Pudelpointer, and the Brittany spaniel—have been generally referred to as "Continentals." In recent years, there has been a movement to drop that reference in favor of the term "versatile gun dogs," a term that more accurately reflects the multipurpose aspects for which these breeds were originated.

Of all of the above, the only breed that does not, in my opinion, fit neatly by temperament and general usage into the versatile gun dog category is the Brittany spaniel. But since geographically he qualifies as a continental, he must be included among the versatiles.

The German shorthaired pointer is officially sponsored in the United States by the German Shorthaired Pointer Club of America, a member breed club of the American Kennel Club. In addition to registration in the A.K.C., many shorthairs are also registered with the American Field Publishing Company's Field Dog Stud Book.

SUMMARY

GERMAN SHORTHAIRED POINTER	(From working field stock.)
TYPE	Pointing breed.
WEIGHT	55 to 70 pounds (average 60 pounds).
HEIGHT AT WITHERS	23 to 25 inches.
COAT TYPE	Shorthaired.
COLOR	In the most desirable specimens, the primary color is white; secondary color (patched and moderately ticked) is liver. Some individuals show far more liver than white.
TAIL	Docked to about 6-inch length.
MATURITY	12 to 14 months.
DISPOSITION	Mild mannered and gentle, if somewhat aloof with strangers;

make good house dogs where space permits.

GAME BIRD SPECIALTIES
Ring-necked pheasants, woodcock, ruffed grouse (and on shooting preserve quail, pheasant, and chukar partridge).

HUNTING RANGE
Can be found in various types, from close to medium-close to medium-wide. But the average and most popular type of shorthairs are of moderately close range and deliberate pace.

TRAINABILITY RATING
Usually attentive, the average shorthairs learn quickly and develop fairly early if given the proper opportunities. Can take and usually require firm discipline to establish good control.

OTHER REMARKS
Like most of the versatile hunting dogs, shorthairs take readily to retrieving, even from water if not too chilly temperature; has strong pointing instinct; easily groomed coat.

THE VIZSLA

If age and beauty were the principal criteria for importing a gun dog to these shores, the vizsla most certainly would qualify 100 percent. Although new, relatively speaking, to North America, the vizsla boasts more seniority on the international scene than any of the other hunting breeds of dogs, with the exception of certain members of the hound group.

The vizsla has a hunting style similar to the German shorthaired pointer's. In common with all of the versatile hunting dogs, his job in the field is to seek, find, and point game birds and, later, after the quarry has been downed by the gun, to retrieve tenderly to hand.

A native of Hungary, the vizsla was developed for hunting birds, rabbits, and hares on the expansive stretches of the region's grassy plains, about 900 to 1,000 years ago, according to some authorities. Well-documented proof, in the form of ancient records and artwork, indicates that the Magyar warriors who, in the eighth century, invaded the territory that later became Hungary brought with them hunting dogs strongly resembling the vizsla. Well before the advent of firearms, these dogs were employed to find prey for the hunters' hawks and falcons.

The development and safeguarding of the bloodlines that evolved from the Magyar dogs was restricted to the conquerors and, for many centuries later, to the Hungarian nobility. Only since 1825, when the breed's modern history began, was the vizsla allowed to fall into the hands of persons not noble born. In that year, the Magyar Vizsla Stud Book was established to record and certify pedigrees guaranteeing the continued purity of the breed.

Two World Wars, plus the 1945 invasion of Hungary by the USSR, nearly placed the vizsla in the same category as the dinosaur. Yet, in each instance, a few hundred refugees and their dogs managed escape to several European countries, where the breed not only was saved from extinction, but eventually bred back up to safe numbers.

The first vizslas arrived in North America in 1950, and achieved acceptance for registry in the American Kennel Club in 1960. Since A.K.C. recognition, the "Handsome Hun" has pawed out a permanent, if not deeply rooted, niche among the pointing dog breeds of North America.

Considering the amount of competition from the earlier continental, or versatile breeds, the vizsla has fared about as well as any comparatively new immigrant to North America. The fact that he has been more of a bird dog specialist, and consequently faced less comparison with the so-called all-purpose talents his earlier continental counterparts had to overcome, might have made things a little easier for him.

A shorthaired dog that stands between 21 and 24 inches at the withers, and weighs about 50 to 60 pounds, the average vizsla today is a more streamlined dog than most German shorthairs. He sports a tail docked to about 6 to 8 inches and a cinnamon or reddish gold-colored smooth coat that is easily groomed. While it does not afford as much protection against cold weather or brambly coverts as the longhaired coats of the setter and Brittany spaniel, it proves a definite asset in warm- and even hot-weather hunting. Also, as is the case with the German shorthair, the vizsla approaches rough cover with a more conservative attitude, seldom bulling his way through at a fast, incautious clip that is likely to cut him up.

Essentially, the vizsla is an industrious hunter, fairly slow in pace   47 and seldom working much beyond a long gun-shot from the gunner. Yet, because of his deliberate way of going, coupled with the kind of scenting prowess that would do justice to a good hound, he doesn't very often miss tight-lying game birds that rangier, faster breeds might overlook.

Like all of the versatile hunting breeds, the vizsla shows a good deal of natural retrieving inclination and ability. Normally, he requires only a minimum amount of encouragement to go about his fetching chores eagerly. On crippled birds he displays tenaciousness in trailing and aggressiveness in running them down.

The vizsla is an efficient pheasant dog; at close range, he hunts by relying upon a combination of body scent and foot scent. When he establishes a solid point, the bird is not so likely to make good his escape by running before the hunter can get to his dog. Moreover, if the vizsla does inadvertently flush a running cock bird, it often is within shootable distance from the hunter.

Woodcock, because they tend to lie well to a pointing dog, are very easily handled by the "Handsome Hun." Ruffed grouse and ring-necks are also generally huntable with a good vizsla. However, due to his limited range and modest pace, the vizsla could not be recommended for hunting most covey birds, such as bobwhite quail, sage grouse, or—ironically—Hungarian partridge, except where these birds are in such unusual abundance that bevies could virtually be tripped over.

In common with most of the other versatile breeds, the vizsla is not a very stylish hunter. Lack of a full-length tail detracts from any dog's way of going, as well as from his regalness and intensity on

---

Above:
The vizsla, one of the oldest pointing dogs in the world, is fairly new to North America. An industrious hunter, he is grouped with the other so-called versatile hunting dogs. Photo by Jerome Knap.
Below, left:
While his shorthaired coat doesn't give as much protection against cold weather and rough cover as that of the longhaired breeds, the vizsla adapts well to most climates and hunts heavy cover with a more cautious attitude. Photo courtesy of Marion I. Coffman, Cariad Kennels, Weston, Conn.
Below, right:
Most vizslas possess scenting prowess that does justice to a good hound. This nine-week-old pup has already learned to nose out his favorite rug in the den. Photo by Judge and Mrs. John F. Lyons.

point; the fact that foot scent receives so much attention, keeping the dog's head low as he runs, also diminishes his attractiveness. Yet, as most supporters of the versatiles are quick to point out, a hunter can't put stylishness in his game pocket.

Extremely alert and intelligent, the vizsla learns his lessons quickly, if he's trained and handled properly. Treat a vizsla the way some owners do a German shorthair—with gruff tones and heavy hand—and you can forget the whole thing. Conversely, give him heaps of praise and affection, and mild rebukes when needed, and your efforts will usually be crowned with success. Definitely sensi-

---

Opposite, above:
Seldom a breathtaking stylist either running or on point, the vizsla normally devotes a great deal of time to working on foot scent. Here, however, this young vizsla is styled into a very classy point by his pretty owner. Photo by Vern D. Brand.
Opposite, below:
Very alert and intelligent, the vizsla can learn his lessons quickly, if trained and handled properly. Honoring his bracemate's point is something this well-conformed vizsla has learned. Photo by William B. Gilbert, courtesy of Marion I. Coffman.
Below:
The average vizsla is a good family companion with a highly protective instinct. Photo by Judge and Mrs. John F. Lyons.

tive in nature, the vizsla nearly always responds to gentleness and affection. An excellent family companion, he has a highly honed protective instinct and can become surprisingly sharp with strange dogs and persons, if they seem to pose any threat to his home and family.

In view of the vizsla's companionableness and protectiveness, he really does better indoors than when kept outside in a backyard kennel. When obtained from field breeding, which is the only kind you should consider, the average vizsla normally is sedate enough to keep indoors, despite his moderately large size.

Official sponsor of the breed in the United States is the Vizsla Club of America, Inc., a member club of the American Kennel Club. In addition to being registered in the A.K.C., many vizslas, especially those of essentially working ancestry, are registered in the American Field Publishing Company's Field Dog Stud Book.

SUMMARY

VIZSLA	(From working field stock.)
TYPE	Pointing breed.
WEIGHT	50 to 60 pounds (average 55 pounds).
HEIGHT AT WITHERS	21 to 24 inches.
COAT TYPE	Shorthaired.
COLOR	Cinnamon to reddish gold.
TAIL	Docked to about 6-inch length.
MATURITY	12 months.
DISPOSITION	Gentle and affectionate with family, highly protective, thus often sharp with strangers; makes good house pet and alert watch dog.
GAME BIRD SPECIALTIES	Woodcock, ring-necked pheasants, ruffed grouse (shooting preserve quail, pheasant, and chukar partridge).
HUNTING RANGE	Almost exclusively a close-working dog, occasional individuals can be found that range to medium-close; pace is usually moderate.
TRAINABILITY RATING	Very alert and intelligent, but sensitive; need much praise and persuasive handling; unresponsive to brusque approach.

OTHER REMARKS	Generally take naturally to retrieving; water work included, if not too cool; extra good scenting abilities; easily groomed coat; good hot-weather hunter.

THE WIREHAIRED POINTING GRIFFON

One of the most unusual of all the versatile hunting breeds, the wirehaired pointing griffon is also the least likely to be perceived as a "bird dog" by those unfamiliar with the breed. Probably, he's among the least likely to win any beauty contests, either. Out of our six pointing dog candidates, he'd doubtless come in seventh in the looks department. But, obviously, he has to have something going for him. Besides being about as affable and tractable as any hunting dog can be, the typical griff offers the gunner a number of distinctive qualities and characteristics definitely worth considering.

Like the rest of the versatile hunting breeds, the wirehaired pointing griffon is required to scout ahead, locate, and point game birds for the gun. Once the bird is flushed and dropped by the gun, the griff must mark his fall and then, on command, fetch it with tender-mouthed care to the waiting gunner. If required, the griff will eagerly enter water to retrieve a downed bird, as will any of the versatiles.

One of the breed's notable assets is his bristly, medium-length coat, steel or whitish gray in color, and splotched with chestnut patches, under which lies a short, heavy secondary coat. If properly textured—that is, hard and wiry—his outer coat wards off burrs and briars and requires very little grooming. Too soft a top coat, however, and those same burrs and other foreign matter will collect and stick on the griff like beggar's lice on cashmere socks.

The chief advantage of the griff's steel-wool pelage and dense undercoat is the virtual impunity it provides him against really cold weather and very chilly water, as well as the worst types of cover imaginable. There is very little cover that the griff is not able, or usually willing, to enter in search of game birds.

Unflagging faith and sincere dedication highlighted the ingredients that went into the original development of the wirehaired pointing griffon. A Dutch sportsman named E. K. Korthals was the undisputed father of the breed. The son of a well-to-do professional banker and amateur cattle breeder, Korthals' preference for sporting dogs over bovines eventually forced him to leave the comfort and security of his father's home in Holland. Emigrating to Germany, he   53 continued his breeding experiments with some of the rough-coated griffons he had brought along from home.

Fragmentary evidence indicates that Korthals worked into his cross-breeding efforts some otterhound, spaniel, setter, and, possibly, German shorthaired pointer blood. Later, in the 1880s, moving from Germany to France, he culminated his experiments, contented that he had brought to perfection the new gun dog breed he had started out to produce.

The year 1887 saw the first wirehaired pointing griffon imported here and registered by the American Kennel Club. However, additional griffons, at least in numbers worth mentioning, did not arrive in North America until after 1900. Not much of a threat to the traditional and well-ensconced pointers and setters here at that time, the griff just bumbled along, barely holding his own for the next four-and-a-half decades. Then, shortly after the end of World War II, with the establishment of the Wirehaired Pointing Griffon Club of America, the scraggly pointer began attracting enough supporters to focus some attention on the breed.

Although the griff has never rivaled the other principal Continental imports, he has achieved a reasonable measure of the attention he deserves. For many years, he had to compete here mainly as a pointer of upland birds, in a totally ridiculous comparison with the well-established traditional pointers and setters. Even though he cannot compare in range, speed, or style with these specialistic upland bird-hunting breeds, anymore than his water work—doubtless the best of all the versatile hunting breeds—can be stacked up against such fantastic performers in water as the Chesapeake Bay or the Labrador retrievers, nevertheless he is a dog that can do a highly serviceable job of finding, pointing, and retrieving upland birds for

---

Above:
Looking not at all like a bird dog, the wirehaired pointing griffon nevertheless has a lot going for him—affable nature, close, deliberate working style, and distinctive appearance. Photo courtesy of the Wirehaired Pointing Griffon Club of America.
Below, left:
The griff's steel-wool pelage and dense undercoat allow him to work with impunity in virtually any kind of cover. Photo courtesy of the Wirehaired Pointing Griffon Club of America.
Below, right:
The scraggly pointing dog has the kind of temperament that makes him practically knock himself out to please an owner he adores.

Photo courtesy of the Wirehaired Pointing Griffon Club of America.

the gun. He is very definitely the closest working, and about the slowest, most deliberate pointing breed available in North America. For many hunters this easy pace and thoroughness prove to be ideal. Since he seldom ranges fast or far, he is easily controlled and takes naturally to the most casual sort of handling by his owner.

By and large, the griff is so eager to please that he will practically knock himself out for a few words of praise, a pat on the head, and a bit of affectionate encouragement. Finding a hunting breed that seeks a closer relationship with master and family would be difficult, indeed.

On woodcock, since they generally lie so tight to a pointing dog, the griff can vie with any dog that stands his game. Ring-necked pheasants and grouse behave about as well for the griff as for most of the other close-to-medium-close working pointing breeds. Birds that inhabit marshy lands and bogs, such as jacksnipe and rails, are easily hunted with the slow, careful, sharp-nosed griffon. And his natural proclivity for retrieving from water adds immensely to the griffon's usefulness in the sort of sloppy cover and conditions that would tend to discourage almost any other pointing breed.

Obviously, however, the wirehaired pointing griffon's restricted range and pace preclude a high degree of practical efficiency on widely scattered bevy-type birds that frequent big, open country, such as bobwhite quail, Hungarian partridge, sage grouse, and sharptails or pinnated grouse.

Inasmuch as the wirehaired pointing griffon, like most of the versatiles, really can't compete against the traditional bird dog specialists in pointing dog field trials, his popularity has been won the hard way. In recent years, however, since the formation of the North American Versatile Hunting Dog Association, the griff and his other

Above:
A training session afield finds this griff pointing staunchly as his owner prepares to flush bobwhite quail. Photo courtesy of the Wirehaired Pointing Griffon Club of America.
Center:
Like all of the Continental, or versatile hunting, breeds, the wirehaired pointing griffon has a docked tail. Photo courtesy of the Wirehaired Pointing Griffon Club of America.
Below:
A natural affinity for retrieving and swimming makes the griff a truly versatile gun dog. Here, a wirehaired pointing griffon fetches a canvas retrieving dummy from an inland pond. Photo courtesy of the Wirehaired Pointing Griffon Club of America.

Puppies are always cute, but if you're interested in getting a good griff for field use, contact the breed club secretary for a list of breeders of approved litters. Photo courtesy of the Wirehaired Pointing Griffon Club of America.

58

European counterparts have been competing successfully among themselves, in field trials patterned largely after those held in Europe.

These NAVHDA trials include tests of the dogs' ability to retrieve on land and from water, as well as to find and point birds for the gun. The NAVHDA tests seek to compare breeds of similar origins, purposes, and styles, and promote them not as specialists but, rather, as hunting dogs designed for a variety of functions afield. NAVHDA is trying to establish a proper niche for breeds of the Continental type and to judge them according to more realistically applicable standards.

The wirehaired pointing griffon stands about 21 to 23 inches high at the withers and weighs between 50 and 65 pounds. This is a fairly big-boned, husky dog, often stockier appearing than he actually is because of his generous coat. Like all of the Continental breeds, his tail is always docked to about one-third of its natural length, or approximately 6 to 8 inches. This breed is temperamentally well suited to sharing indoor quarters with the family. His docile, sociable disposition makes for an always pleasant man-dog relationship.

If your home is not unduly small, the griff's generally placid nature minimizes the problems normally associated with a big, active dog. Besides, as a kennel dog, the griff, like most of the versatiles, leaves lots to be desired. As far as the griffon is concerned, if he can't be with his own boss and family, he'd almost rather be nowhere.

Anyone considering the purchase of wirehaired pointing griffon should be extremely cautious about his source of supply. In the past few years, a good deal of indiscriminate breeding of griffons has taken place. Persons more interested in producing dogs for the show ring, or in making a quick buck, seldom bother to breed for the essential qualities of the true, working field dog. Anyone seeking to buy a griff should contact the Wirehaired Pointing Griffon Club of America to obtain the names and addresses of breeders of approved litters. Only by so doing can you be assured that the puppy offered you for sale will possess all the necessary field potentials that his breeder and the approval committee can reasonably and conscientiously predict. For such information, contact Ms. Kathryn Haberkorn, 36340 Hillside Lane, Lebanon, OR 97355.

Most wirehaired pointing griffons are registered with the American Kennel Club, although an increasing number are also registered with the Field Dog Stud Book.

SUMMARY

WIREHAIRED POINTING GRIFFON	(From working field stock.)
TYPE	Pointing breed.
WEIGHT	50 to 65 pounds (average 58 pounds).
HEIGHT AT WITHERS	21 to 23 inches.
COAT TYPE	Medium length wirehaired.
COLOR	Primary color is steel gray or dirty white; secondary coloring is splotches of chestnut.
TAIL	Docked to 6- to 8-inch length.
MATURITY	18 to 22 months.
DISPOSITION	Docile, affectionate, very eager to please; makes excellent house pet; poor kennel dog.
GAME BIRD SPECIALTIES	Woodcock, ring-necked pheasant, ruffed grouse, jacksnipe, rails (both sora and clapper), (shooting preserve quail, pheasant, and chukar partridge).
HUNTING RANGE	Very close working dog of slow, thorough type; in fact, closest and easiest paced of all North American pointing breeds.
TRAINABILITY RATING	Exceptionally willing worker that shows great enthusiasm to learn, as long as his progress seems to please owner; he is somewhat sensitive to owner's moods and needs praise and encouragement; harsh treatment should be avoided.
OTHER REMARKS	Not a good choice for open country where well-scattered covey birds require a wide-ranging dog; too soft a coat should be avoided; check Wirehaired Pointing Griffon Club for Breeding Committee-approved litters.

CHAPTER 3

FOUR FLUSHING BREED CANDIDATES

Having examined the six pointing breeds on our list of ten prime gun dog candidates, we're ready now to consider the four breeds that flush rather than point upland birds for the gun. It should be noted that, technically speaking, only two of the four—the English springer spaniel and the American water spaniel—are true flushing specialists; the other two, by origin and classification, are waterfowl retrieving breeds that have found practical usage as pinch hit flushing dogs in the uplands.

THE ENGLISH SPRINGER SPANIEL

If the ring-necked pheasant had but a single wish, doubtless it would be to live in a world uninhabited by the English springer spaniel. There are countless hunters, however, who are just as glad that the world *is* well populated by springers; such sportsmen have two loves: ring-neck hunting and springer spaniels with which to hunt.

Too often it's difficult to say, with honesty and conviction, that this product or that item is the greatest. Yet, it's easy to state unequivocally that the English springer spaniel is the greatest, the most efficient pheasant hunting dog in the world. And anyone caring to dispute the statement would be well advised to restrict his opinions to springer enthusiasts considerably smaller than himself.

The springer's basic job in the uplands is to seek, find, and flush game birds quickly and decisively—but only within killing range of the gun. By quartering to the front and sides of the gunner, the properly trained springer will search out both airborne body scent and ground foot scent; then he'll indicate his quarry's proximity in a blur of stub-tailed vibrations that cease only after he has pushed his bird skyward. Immediately sitting, or "hupping," at the flush, he'll await both the shot and the order to fetch, if indeed the shot has produced a dead bird.

The earliest written documentation of the spaniel's hunting style was found in the previously mentioned *Le Livre de la Chasse* (*The Book of the Hunt*) by French nobleman Gaston de Foix. Written in 1387, the volume tells of the spaniel's ground-quartering technique, running ahead of the hunters and their hawks and falcons, as well as of the dog's swimming abilities and retrieving from water.

About 200 years later, in his book *Of Englishe Dogges,* Dr. John Caius more fully elaborated on the spaniels and divided them into two different varieties: those used on land and those most proficient in water. The former were even further broken down into "springers," dogs that sprang or flushed game for the sight hounds or hunting hawks, and "setting spaniels," which pointed or "set" game for the nets. It was these "setting spaniels" that were generally believed to have formed the foundation for the three breeds eventually called "setters."

Land spaniels of the flushing persuasion differed greatly in size and sometimes were named for the game on which they specialized. Most often used to hunt woodcock, the smaller flushing spaniels were called "cocking" or "cocker" spaniels. But, because bloodlines were so indiscriminately commingled, with no thought given to uniformity, a dog might be called a cocker for the first year of his life and, after adding more size, end up as a springer at maturity.

Above:

The English springer spaniel is acclaimed by most flushing-breed enthusiasts as the greatest pheasant-hunting dog in the world. Here, one of the bench show types—Ch. Loresta's Storm King—evidences the breed's beauty. Photo by Henry C. Schley, courtesy of Edward and Lillian Stapp, Fontana, Calif.

Below:

A natural propensity for fetching makes the average field-bred springer a good retriever. Seldom do springers have to be force-trained to retrieve.

Sportsmen began looking more seriously at the springer as spaniel field trials came into vogue in England around the turn of the twentieth century; in 1902 separate classifications were attained for the springer, cocker, and clumber spaniels. With this came the proper attention to selective breeding that marked the real beginning of the springer's modern history.

The first purebred springers found their way into North America in 1907. Their numbers were insignificant, and since the earlier imported setters and pointers so held sway, the breed created scant attention. But, through the efforts of a Canadian, Eudore Chevrier, who imported, trained, bred, and sold springers in substantial numbers during the early 1920s, the breed began establishing a firm foundation in North America. After the founding of the English Springer Spaniel Field Trial Association in 1924, and the holding of its initial trial at Fisher's Island, the springer and his steadfast admirers grew stronger and more numerous with each passing season.

Today's English springer spaniel, like so many of the hunting breeds in North America, can be divided into two varieties—field type and show type. Since it is the former that the sportsman is interested in, reasonable care must be taken to make certain the puppy selected emanates from field trial and hunting ancestry. The show springer is a handsome animal, usually weighing better than 50 pounds, but he just doesn't have the fiery drive needed in the field. His working compatriot, however, has all the physical and instinctive attributes to get the job done successfully and look flashy while doing it. The average field dog normally weighs somewhere between 40 and 50 pounds, stands from 18 to 22 inches high at the withers, and has a tail docked to about 8 inches long.

The springer's silky longhaired coat of white, patched with black or liver, is as eye-pleasing as it is functional, its feathering providing just the right touch of jauntiness, and its length and thickness the necessary shield against weather and heavy brush. Generously white, it makes him easy to keep track of in upland coverts and shadowy swamps.

The same longhaired coat that so well insulates him from both chilly temperatures and rigorous covers has the disadvantage of collecting burrs, twigs, and other bits of foreign matter. Unless the

His longhaired coat insulates him from chilly temperatures and the punishment of rigorous covers, but it will be a while before this springer pup encounters either. Photo by Mr. and Mrs. Ray Adell, Lleda Kennels, Huntington, N.Y.

Four Flushing Breed Candidates

hunter carries along a stripping comb or other detangling tool for periodic use during a day's outing, he often can be faced with a horrendous chore come evening, when he least feels in the mood for tackling it.

The springer is without peer on ring-necked pheasants, but as long as he is reliably trained to hunt and flush no more than 40 yards from the gun, he can also be used on a wide variety of game birds and even on rabbits. He does especially well in working ruffed grouse and woodcock, although using him to hunt the latter bird, which generally lies so well to a pointing dog, seems to offend the sensibilities of the old-line woodcock hunter. Nonetheless, from a purely practical standpoint, the springer will put woodcock in the bag, assuming his owner can hit the long-billed twisters.

Bobwhite quail, while hardly the springer's specialty, can be hunted with reasonable success in small fields that can be quartered quickly with the dog working within gun range at all times. However, the springer cannot be expected to function efficiently on covey birds such as the various valley, mountain, and desert quails of the big open areas.

Although lacking the speed and agility of the retriever breeds in water, the springer performs quite well as a swimmer and can be expected to fetch dead or crippled birds that are dropped into or across bodies of water. Where water temperatures don't fall too low, the springer can also be used to fetch waterfowl, doing a moderately good to excellent job as a duck dog.

Practically any member of the breed that comes from proven field ancestry can be depended upon to possess all the necessary qualifications to become a good bird dog when properly trained. Highly affectionate and very gentle, the springer usually takes to training with spirited eagerness. A firmness that establishes authority in a skillful rather than heavy-handed fashion will generally get best results, for the springer is a somewhat soft, sensitive dog, inclined toward sulkiness if disciplined too harshly. Handled adroitly, though, he makes an attentive pupil that learns quickly and retains his lessons well, seldom requiring more than brush-up review before each new hunting season.

Unless there is really good reason not to, the springer should be

---

Highly affectionate and very gentle, the springer spaniel usually takes to training with spirited eagerness. This old boy figures he's earned some time out after helping hunter Bob Elman bring a big cock pheasant to bag. Photo by Leonard Lee Rue III.

given house pet status. Although he can adapt to kennel life if he has to, he far prefers sharing indoor quarters with his owner and the family. The owner who unnecessarily keeps his springer kenneled misses untold companionship from a breed that is as captivatingly warm and loyal in the home as he is bold and aggressive in the field.

The springer is sponsored in the United States by the National English Springer Spaniel Field Trial Association, a member club of the American Kennel Club. Since both bench and field bred springers are registered with the A.K.C., the hunter should exercise some caution in making certain the pup he buys comes from ancestry with suitable hunting field credentials.

While the springer can adapt to kennel life if he has to, he far prefers living indoors with his owner and family. Hopefully, each of this quartet will acquire an owner who'll share the hacienda. Photo by Edward and Lillian Stapp.

SUMMARY

ENGLISH SPRINGER SPANIEL	(From working field stock.)
TYPE	Flushing breed.
WEIGHT	40 to 50 pounds.
HEIGHT AT WITHERS	18 to 22 inches.
COAT TYPE	Long, flat, or slightly wavy and soft.
COLOR	Primary color is white; secondary color is black or liver patches with some ticking.
TAIL	Docked to about 8-inch length.
MATURITY	18 months.
DISPOSITION	Gentle and affectionate, although somewhat sensitive; makes ideal house pet.
GAME BIRD SPECIALTIES	Ring-necked pheasant tops the list, but also very effective on woodcock and ruffed grouse; limited use on bobwhite quail in restricted covers (shooting preserve quail, pheasant, and chukar partridge).
HUNTING RANGE	All flushing breeds must be trained to work within shotgun range, generally flushing quarry under 30 yards but never more than 40 from the gun.
TRAINABILITY RATING	Spirited student with strong desire to please; needs tactful handling to produce consistent control without detracting from naturally happy style of working.
OTHER REMARKS	A highly versatile gun dog that also makes an excellent home companion; handy-sized; good retriever on land and from moderately cool water; fine choice for heavy cover work; coat has tendency to pick up burrs.

THE LABRADOR RETRIEVER

As a specialist at fetching downed ducks and geese from rivers, lakes, ponds, and swamps, the Labrador retriever has earned the reputation of being the nation's most popular water dog. Only the Chesapeake Bay retriever might be considered more at home and possessed of greater stamina in the water than the Labrador, but the Chessy's popularity rating comes nowhere close to that of retriever-dom's ruling monarch.

Whether as a field trial contender or a working duck dog, the Lab has an indisputable stranglehold on first place in the world of water-fowl breeds. Yet, it is not as a duck dog but rather as a flusher of upland birds that the Labrador has been selected for our list of ten prime bird dog candidates.

In the uplands, the Lab is expected to perform essentially the same function as a springer, seeking and finding game birds by a combination of aerial and ground scent. Casting from side to side in front of the gun, he'll lock in on fresh scent, begin wagging his long tail with increasing fervor, and bore in hard until his feathered target takes to the air. At the flush, which should, of course, be inside scatter-gun killing range, the Lab should "Hup" and remain sitting until the shot is fired and he receives the order to fetch a dead bird, or, in the event of a miss, resume hunting.

Since retrieving is the breed's specialty, the Lab is superbly adept at marking fallen birds and equally reliable in running down cripples. Seldom does even a wing-tipped pheasant—one of the fastest-running game birds around—escape a good Labrador, to die a lingering death or become fox bait.

Contrary to his name, the breed did not originate in Labrador. Canine historians trace it to Newfoundland and an ancestry known there in the early 1800s as the St. John's Newfoundland. The St. John's dogs were considerably smaller than the Newfie and had shorter, smoother coats. Although they saw some service as water-fowl retrievers, the St. John's dogs earned their chow primarily in assisting the fishermen by swimming with ropes from ship to ship and ship to shore.

Brought to England about 1820 at the behest of the second Earl of Malmesbury, the St. John's dogs were consistently referred to as Labrador retrievers by the Earl and renowned British sportsman Colonel Hawker, who were the breed's staunchest supporters. Both gentlemen did much to popularize the "Labradors" as excellent swimmers and retrievers.

In the years that followed, even though the second Earl of Mal-

Gentle of disposition, alert of mind and captivatingly sociable is the Labrador retriever. With proper, patient training, he can be taught to be a proficient flusher of upland-game birds. Photo by Mrs. James Warwick, Lockerbie Kennels, Little Silver, N.J.

mesbury kept the breeding of his dogs relatively pure, other breeders outcrossed their Labs. Commonplace retriever breeds of the time, such as the curly coated and flat coated retrievers, are believed to have been utilized, and an occasional setter (probably Gordon) and pointer may also have contributed to the breed that has become today's Labrador retriever.

Officially recognized by the English Kennel Club in 1903, the Lab   71 found his way back into North America in very limited numbers not long afterward. But it was not until the late 1920s that the breed arrived in really countable quantities. In 1931 the Labrador Club of America was founded and, later that same year, the first licensed Labrador retriever field trial in America took place in the town of Chester, New York.

Largely through the efforts of a small group of well to do sportsmen in the Northeast, who bred good field and show stock and

Opposite, above:
The Lab's specialty is retrieving and that makes a good part of the job of training him a lot easier. This Lab picks up a pheasant to bring back to his boss.
Opposite, below:
The Labrador retriever's agility on land qualifies him very well for work in the uplands. Keeping him within gun range is vital at all times if he is to become a practical flushing dog.
Below:
Labs come in three different colors, the most popular being black, with yellow next, and chocolate a distant third.

campaigned their dogs both in field trials and in the show ring, the Labrador began attracting attention among sportsmen during the 1930s and 1940s. Although the breed's work as nonslip retrievers (dogs kept at heel until ordered to fetch a dead or crippled bird found by pointer or spaniel and dropped by the gun) found favor in the British Isles, such use by the average sportsman here never achieved great popularity. Obviously, most American hunters could afford neither the time nor the money to keep and train, or have professionally trained, two hunting dogs of highly different specialties.

But, as a retriever of ducks and geese, the Lab quickly eclipsed virtually all of the other retriever breeds in North America. By the 1950s retriever trials had become dominated by Labradors, with golden retrievers running a poor second and Chesapeake Bay dogs almost as scarce as dinosaurs.

For a few years, when waterfowl seasons and bag limits were whittled down to the bare bones, the popularity of all the retriever breeds in the United States dropped accordingly. But the discovery that the fetch dogs could also be utilized as pinch-hit flushing dogs in the uplands served as a real boon, boosting once more the Lab's as well as the golden's and the other retrievers' acceptance among active gun dog owners.

Today's Labrador retriever in America has changed somewhat from the earlier importations of the 1930s. He now tends toward a bit more legginess and a somewhat more svelte overall appearance. Standing about 24 inches high at the withers and weighing between 60 and 75 pounds, he has a short, dense, smooth coat that readily turns away water and chilly weather and generally sheds burrs, sticktights, and twig bits as slickly as patent leather. Solid black is the color most often seen in the Labrador, with yellow the second most common, and chocolate running a distant third. He carries a full-length round tail, thick and otterlike at the base and tapering moderately toward the end.

Besides his natural fetching instinct, which more than pays his way in the uplands, the Lab has both the temperament and the physique to qualify him for work as a flushing dog. He is eager and intelligent and once he understands that you want him to seek and flush birds, rather than merely fetching them, he will usually hunt sedulously. However, since flushing dog work is not the breed's longtime primary specialty, most Labs cannot be expected to approach the task as quickly or with the same instinctive verve as a springer spaniel.

74   Yet, given the proper opportunities and patient encouragement,

practically any Labrador can be successfully trained to hunt within shotgun range and do a serviceable job of flushing birds for the gun.

Pheasants doubtless make up the lion's share of upland birds the Lab helps put in the game bag. But ruffed grouse and woodcock are not far behind and, in fact, the Lab can generally prove equal to hunting any game bird considered normal quarry for a spaniel.

In common with all breeds that flush their game, the Labrador is apt to be least practical on birds that covey—such as bobwhite, mountain, valley, and desert quails; chukar and Hungarian partridges; sage hens and prairie chickens. Certainly there are bound to be some hunters who'll disagree, citing years of experience with one or more of these game birds that only a Labrador could handle. Naturally, exceptions prove the rule, but bear in mind that we are not considering the exceptions here.

If the Labrador has any disadvantages as a flusher of upland birds, one is hard pressed to find them. True, a majority of the breed is solid black, a color not too readily visible in shadowy thickets. But because of the dog's size, full-length tail, and the necessity to work

If space permits, the Lab makes a fine house dog. Yet, if he must be kenneled, start him out at a young age. Photo by Mrs. James Warwick.

close to the gun, visibility is not too much of a problem. About the only disadvantage of the Lab in the uplands is simply the fact that he isn't a springer spaniel—but that is equally true for any other of the flushing breeds.

Gentle of disposition, alert of mind, and captivatingly sociable, the average Labrador is tractable enough for anyone to train and handle. Probably this compliant nature, which generally makes the breed so easy to train, accounts for the Lab's great popularity among women, especially those who actively engage in retriever field trials. As with any breed, there can be found some hardheaded roughnecks that require gentling with methods and techniques a bit stronger than might ordinarily be expected. As a rule, though, such Labs are far from typical representatives of the breed.

Because of his flexible nature, the Lab can be kept in a backyard kennel, either full or part time. But most Labrador owners end up granting their dogs at least some time indoors with the family. The fact that the Lab has the ability to wriggle his way into the hearts, minds, and homes of most of his owners says a great deal for his affability.

The Labrador Retriever Club of America officially sponsors the breed in the United States. Since this is a member club of the American Kennel Club, most Labs are registered with the A.K.C. Some are registered with the Field Dog Stud Book and some with both registries. In buying a Labrador retriever primarily for use in the field and as a house pet, we would recommend that he be chosen from a line incorporating as much field stock as possible. However, in all fairness, a bit of bench show breeding in the average Lab generally will not detract from his field potential to the same extent that such stock might affect the working potentials of other breeds.

SUMMARY

LABRADOR RETRIEVER	(From essentially working field stock.)
TYPE	Retriever used as flushing breed.
WEIGHT	60 to 75 pounds.
HEIGHT AT WITHERS	24 inches.
COAT TYPE	Short, dense and smooth.
COLOR	Solid black is most common; solid yellow next most common; chocolate seen only occasionally.

TAIL	Full-length round, otterlike at base and tapering moderately toward its end.
MATURITY	18 to 24 months.
DISPOSITION	Docile and affectionate; makes good house pet in roomy quarters.
GAME BIRD SPECIALTIES	Good for pheasants and is effective on woodcock and ruffed grouse; very limited value for use on bobwhite quail or other covey birds; except to retrieve downed birds (shooting preserve pheasants, chukar partridge, and single quail).
HUNTING RANGE	All flushing breeds, or retrievers used as such, must be trained to work within shotgun range, generally flushing quarry under 30 yards but never more than 40 from the gun.
TRAINABILITY RATING	Very responsive pupil with strong desire to please; can take punishment in stride and continue working happily; probably one of the easiest hunting breeds to train for serviceable work.
OTHER REMARKS	A proficient and very adaptable gun dog that can be used effectively in the uplands and as a highly developed retriever on land or in water; fine companion afield or at home.

THE GOLDEN RETRIEVER

The golden retriever is the second most popular fetch dog breed in North America. Like the Lab, the golden is a true waterfowling specialist, earning his daily due primarily as a duck and goose hunter's dog. Also, like the Lab, he has become a popular favorite of the retriever field trialer, as well as of the bench show fancier.

But it is not as a water worker that we are concerned with the golden here. Instead, he has been chosen as a pinch-hit flusher of upland game birds and, as such, the golden probably boasts a bit more in his heritage for the job than does the Lab.

Functioning as a spaniel in the uplands, the golden is expected to conduct a diligent search for birds, utilizing both body and foot scent to locate his quarry. Quartering ground to the front and sides of the gunner, he'll tune in on any hot effluvia, trail it to its source and, vigorously flailing his plumed tail, roust the bird into the air. With the target airborne in easy gun range, the golden must sit, or "Hup," to flush and wait in that position, intent on marking the bird at the shot. If the bird has been downed, he will fetch it back tenderly on command, otherwise he'll begin—again on command—his assiduous quest for additional game.

Although the origins of many of today's sporting breeds have long been obscured and are usually pieced together with scanty facts and gobs of speculation, the golden's true beginning has been documented, albeit only in recent years. For almost a century, a story that might well have done credit to an early day press agent was passed off as the factual and official history of the golden's origin. Because it was a good story, zestfully imaginative and thoroughly appealing, it went completely unquestioned. Despite its obviously interesting aspects, we've decided not to repeat it here, in the hope that, by omission, it will die a natural death and no longer becloud the real origin of the golden retriever breed.

The true story of the golden's beginning was first revealed in England in 1952, when Lord Ilchester turned up the handwritten breeding records kept by his great uncle, Lord Tweedmouth, who originated the breed in the 1860s. Lord Tweedmouth started with a dog named Nous that was the only yellow puppy in a litter of black wavy-coated retrievers, a breed now known as flat-coated retrievers.

Next, Tweedmouth bred Nous to Belle, a Tweed water spaniel that was a pale liverish-colored breed indigenous to the area of the Tweed River of Scotland. From this mating several yellow pups were produced, two of which Tweedmouth retained at his Guisachan Kennels and subsequently bred back to a Tweed water spaniel. Later crosses were introduced, among them a couple of black retrievers—presumably wavy-coated, flat-coated, or Labrador retrievers—and an Irish setter.

In the 1890s, Tweedmouth finally succeeded in establishing a breed of uniform type and color. Pups from these early matings eventually created three other strains of the breed that were destined

The golden retriever can legitimately be termed the most beautiful of the fetch-dog breeds. Amiable, affectionate, and alert, he makes a nimble flush dog in the uplands. Photo by Jerome Knap, courtesy of Jim Irwin.

to become officially recognized as golden retrievers by the Kennel Club of England in 1913.

The earliest goldens to reach North America are believed to have been brought into Canada, around the turn of the century, by retired British Army officers. It was not until about 1912 that the breed reached the United States in anything approaching substantial numbers. Even at that, the golden did not receive official recognition and acceptance as a separate breed in the Canadian and American Kennel Clubs until 1927 and 1932 respectively.

Without doubt, the greatest field trial golden ever seen in, North America was Rip, owned, trained, and handled by Paul Bakewell III of St. Louis, Missouri. Rip was the first golden ever to earn the title of Field Trial Champion in the United States, winning the coveted crown in 1939, only a year after the formation here of the Golden Retriever Club of America.

In 1941, another golden, King Midas of Woodend, outshone all the other entrants and won top laurels in the premiere running of the National Retriever Championship. Suddenly, the American gun dog fraternity became very much aware that a breed called the golden retriever was here to stay.

If Labradors dominate the retriever trials—and indeed the record bears out the fact—the golden is nonetheless a persistent contender. Although never the equal of the rough and rugged Chesapeake Bay dog in frigid water, the golden can usually handle virtually any reasonable retrieve from water. However, when it comes to flushing dog work on land, a good golden must be given a slight edge over a good Labrador.

Owing to his early ancestry, which included not only some Gordon setter blood (from the wavy-coated retriever) but also at least one known infusion of Irish setter in Lord Tweedmouth's foundation stock, the golden almost always exhibits extra sharp scenting powers. And, although he must be properly trained to limit his quartering

---

Above:
His natural intelligence and eagerness to learn contribute immeasurably to the golden's responsiveness to training. Shown here is Ronakers Majestic Blaze. Photo by Kado Marsh, courtesy of Bob and Margaret Risso.
Below:
Since his specialty is retrieving, the golden should be taught the basics, such as taking a line, in order to make him a polished performer. Photo by Jerome Knap, courtesy of Jim Irwin.

to shotgun range, he can generally be relied upon to pick up and successfully unravel the scent trails of upland game birds in woods, fields, and swamps.

The average golden will stand about 23 to 24 inches high at the withers and weigh between 65 and 75 pounds. A generously thick under coat, overlaid with a flat or slightly wavy outer coat of long hair that varies in color from light golden to reddish golden effectively protects the dog from all but the most severe climactic conditions. Ample feathering on the golden's legs, underbelly, and full-length tail give him a setterlike appearance. And the more reddish-colored specimens might easily be taken for faded Irish setters, were it not for the golden's more stocky build.

Pretty as the golden's longhaired coat is, it does present the same burr-gathering tendencies common to the longhaired breeds. Thinning out excessive feathering on the tail, legs, and underbelly—something that would cause the golden's bench show fancier to shudder in horror—can help eliminate the worst of the detangling chores that must be attended to after a day's hunt in the uplands.

What are the upland birds the breed handles best? As is true of

Opposite:
The golden makes an excellent flusher of upland birds, including such species as the chukar partridge, which is found on most commercial shooting preserves. Photo by Jerome Knap.
Below:
Handled adroitly, the golden is an easy breed to train, often displaying the same verve for hunting as this one shows for hitting the water on command to fetch. Photo by Jerome Knap.

both the springer and the Labrador, the golden probably turns in his best work on ring-necked pheasants, pushing them out of cover with enthusiasm almost equal to the springer's. Yet, if the greatest percentage of the breed's upland hunting concentrates on the ring-neck, fair numbers of ruffed grouse and woodcock also are put to flight by the golden.

Like all flushing breeds, the golden is at a distinct disadvantage when used to hunt birds that frequent wide open country. Such species as bobwhite, mountain, valley, and desert quails, chukar and Hungarian partridges, sage hens, and prairie chickens usually require pinning down by a pointing breed, and even that is often a difficult feat when the coveys are spooky. A flushing breed, which is required to hunt within shotgun range, just isn't able to get close enough to such covey birds and still remain within 30 or 40 yards of the gunner.

In personality, the golden can only be called amiable, affectionate, and alert. He is always very gentle and attentive to his human family, making a truly fine, thoroughly trustworthy companion to everyone in the household. Seldom will the average golden display hostility toward other dogs or even strangers, although he makes a vigilant watchdog with the sort of deep, chesty bark that discourages most would-be intruders.

His natural intelligence and eagerness to learn contribute immeasurably to the golden's ability to respond to training. If handled adroitly, there probably is no easier breed to train successfully. But, due to his somewhat soft temperament, the golden does not take to overstrong punishment. Coercion is never the proper solution to teaching a golden anything; the more pressure the trainer applies, the more sulky and less cooperative his pupil becomes. Yet, there is no doubt that the patient, gentle, tactful owner—either male or female—can accomplish wonders with the golden.

The golden is a fair to good kennel dog, adjusting reasonably well to spending most of his time outdoors if placed in a backyard kennel at an early age. But if indoor quarters permit his living in the house, the golden will reward his owner and family with the kind of love, loyalty, and devotion that transcends whatever small degree of inconvenience such arrangement may involve.

The official organization sponsoring the breed in the United States is the Golden Retriever Club of America, a member club of the American Kennel Club. As is true with the Labrador, most goldens are registered with the A.K.C., although some are listed with both the A.K.C. and the Field Dog Stud Book.

SUMMARY

GOLDEN RETRIEVER	(From essentially working field stock.)
TYPE	Retriever used as flushing breed.
WEIGHT	65 to 75 pounds.
HEIGHT AT WITHERS	23 to 24 inches.
COAT TYPE	Long, flat, or slightly wavy outer coat and thick, dense undercoat.
COLOR	Light golden to reddish golden.
TAIL	Full-length, generously feathered.
MATURITY	20 to 26 months.
DISPOSITION	Very gentle, extremely affectionate and devoted, although somewhat soft in temperament; makes wonderful house and companion dog where space permits.
GAME BIRD SPECIALTIES	Good on ring-necks and very adept at flushing woodcock and ruffed grouse; limited value on bobwhite quail or most other covey birds, except for retrieving purposes (shooting preserve pheasants, chukar partridges, and single quail).
HUNTING RANGE	All flushing breeds, or retrievers used as such, must be trained to work within shotgun range, generally flushing quarry under 30 yards, but never more than 40 from the gun.
TRAINABILITY RATING	Intelligent, eager learner, if handled tactfully, with gentle persuasion; never responds to brute force or brusque treatment; properly handled makes one of easiest breeds to train; usually responds well to women trainers.
OTHER REMARKS	Generally has slight edge over Lab in use on upland birds; excellent nose contributes to success in uplands; efficient retriever on land or in water; longhaired coat tends to gather burrs.

THE AMERICAN WATER SPANIEL

The last of our ten prime candidates is the perky little American water spaniel. Being listed last is certainly no reflection on the breed; some breed had to be listed in the final slot, and it just happened to fall to the American to bring up the rear.

The American water spaniel comes about as close to genuine versatility as any breed can—one that, like his very distant cousin, the Brittany spaniel, is easy to house, to kennel, to transport, to care for. Used in the uplands, the American operates as a typical flushing dog, questing the scent of the game birds by quartering from side to side ahead of the gun. Utilizing body or foot scent, or a combination of both, he'll home in on his prey and, with full-length tail wagging feverishly to indicate the game's presence, force it into flight an easy gunshot from his boss. Like all mannerly flush dogs, he'll ''Hup'' as the bird takes wing, gluing his eyes on the target to mark its fall. When the bird is down, the American will, on command, jog out and retrieve it promptly, with soft-mouthed delivery, before the order to find some more starts him hunting eagerly again.

Nominally and technically a spaniel, the American was originated primarily as a retriever of ducks, sometime toward the late 1800s. As one of only two retrievers developed exclusively on our shores, the American was put together in the country around the Fox and Wolf river valleys of central Wisconsin. The breed came about in answer to the need for a dog small enough to operate efficiently out of the skiffs and canoes commonly used in hunting ducks in the region, yet sufficiently rugged to stand the gaff of retrieving large numbers of ducks during a day's hunt.

No one knows, as is so often the case with hunting dogs, exactly which breeds were combined to produce the American water spaniel. However, it is most probable that the foundation stock included the old English water spaniel, now extinct, the curly coated retriever, and the Irish water spaniel.

The late Dr. F. J. Pfeifer of New London, Wisconsin, the man generally acknowledged to have been most responsible for shepherding the breed to purebred status—he registered the first American water spaniel with the United Kennel Club in 1920—vehemently disputed any Irish water spaniel blood in the breed. Thomas Brogden of Rush Lake, Wisconsin, and Karl Hinz of Milwaukee, Wisconsin, two other breeders of the American during the 1930s, did subscribe to the inclusion of Irish water spaniel in the American's heritage.

86   The rugged little spaniel attracted a dedicated core of supporters

late in the 1930s. Led by one of their members, John Scofield of Jonesburg, Missouri, a fresh infusion of interest in the American Water Spaniel Club of America—first formed in 1881—eventually achieved recognition for the breed by the Field Dog Stud Book, in 1938. Acceptance for registry as a purebred by the American Kennel Club followed in 1940.

Although the American was developed principally for duck hunting, his versatility was recognized early on and even in the latter part of the nineteenth century he saw considerable work springing marsh birds in the lowlands and ruffed grouse and rabbits in the uplands. Later, after the successful introduction and spread of the ring-necked pheasant from Oregon's Willamette Valley, the American added this immigrant species to his enlarging repertoire.

A small-to-medium-size breed, the American water spaniel stands about 15 to 18 inches high at the withers and weighs from 25 to 40 pounds. Curly to wavy medium-length hair covers the dog's ears, neck, body, legs, and undocked tail. Definitely not a cobby dog, the

---

The American water spaniel certainly deserves the description, "good things come in small packages." He is only one of two retrievers developed exclusively on U.S. soil. Photo by John Scofield, Jonesburg, Mo.

87

American is built a bit longer in body than his height at shoulder, an asset in many upland bird coverts, where going under may be preferable to trying to crash through or over heavy tangles.

While readily picking up debris in such cover, the dog's dense coat provides excellent protection against thorns and briers and serves equally well in insulating him against cold weather. His solid liver or dark chocolate coloring doesn't make him highly visible to the

---

Opposite, above:
Keen and intelligent, the American is also highly versatile. He eagerly retrieves whatever his boss shoots, be it upland bird or duck. Courtesy: The American Water Spaniel Club, Inc.
Opposite, below:
Firmness, achieved more with vocal than physical chastisement, and tempered with kindliness, generally brings out the best in the perky American. Courtesy: The American Water Spaniel Club, Inc., 18515 Lake George Blvd. NW, Anoka, MN 55303.
Below:
A dense curly to wavy coat affords the American ample protection in cold water or heavy cover. Courtesy: American Water Spaniel Club, Inc.

hunter in dimly lighted thickets, but since, as a flushing breed, he shouldn't venture too far from his handler, his coloration is not a serious handicap.

For a variety of reasons, the American has never achieved the degree of popularity the breed deserves as a versatile hunter, retriever, and companion dog: he is far from a breathtaking beauty, hence, he hasn't much of a bench show following; in field trials the breed is not fast enough or sufficiently spectacular to compete successfully against Labradors and goldens; a great many gunners simply don't even know the American water spaniel exists. And that's a genuine shame, because he is the kind of gun dog that can please a good many of those same sportsmen to whom he is anonymous.

For example, in the uplands his work is at a pace most accurately described as methodical but merry. Hunting much as a springer does, the little American merely moves with less speed, putting him in closer proximity to a hunter who, perhaps because of age or natural preference, progresses at a more leisurely stride. There are untold numbers of sportsmen who fit into this category.

Pheasants would have to be considered the breed's primary game in the uplands. And if anyone is lulled into thinking the American is less than agile while hot ring-neck scent is scorching his nostrils, don't be misled—he'll keep right on the bird's tail until the cackler gets aloft.

Second to the ring-neck for the little spaniel would have to be the migrant woodcock, a bird the American handles expertly in the heavy tag alders so often preferred by old longbill. Ruffed grouse, too, while no pushover for any breed, can be hunted successfully with pretty fair regularity.

As is true of all the flushing breeds, the American must be considered least practical on covey birds in big, open country. Widely scattered birds such as bevies of bobwhite, mountain, valley, and desert quails, chukar and Hungarian partridges, sage hens, and prairie chickens are not the average American water spaniel's meat. However, as an accomplished retriever of game on land, as well as from water, he is frequently used to retrieve covey birds walked up by a hunter and his companions and, of course, in such situations he is also bound to produce an occasional covey on his own.

The American can even be pressed into service pushing up marsh birds, such as sora and clapper rails and jacksnipe, and fetching them back for the gun. He can be taught to spring cottontails and shows no hesitation in retrieving them either. While hardly equal to rough water retrieving tasks, the breed proves an ideal dog for fetching ducks dumped in small lakes, inland potholes, and marshes. And, because of his size, he still makes a good choice for the gunner who enjoys jump shooting from a canoe.

Temperamentally, the American is typically spaniel, affectionate to those close to him and very eager to win their approval. He is an alert, intelligent dog; not only does he learn quickly, but his retentive memory makes the annual refresher course needed by many other gun dog breeds virtually obsolete for most American water spaniels with only a couple of hunting seasons under their belts.

Bright as he is, the American does display the spaniel predisposition toward sullenness if trained and handled too brusquely. Undue force on the trainer's part turns the American off completely, leaving him somber and moody, often for hours, depending on the degree of pressure involved. Firmness, achieved more with vocal than physical chastisement, and tempered with kindliness, normally brings out the best in him.

A fairly good kennel dog, the American is, however, so handy-sized that he should fit conveniently into practically any household. His only possible drawback as an indoor dog might stem from the fact that he has a somewhat oily coat. Yet, if he is brushed and toweled down regularly, this oiliness can easily be kept under control.

The official sponsor of the breed in the United States is the American Water Spaniel Club, a member club of the American Kennel Club. The breed is also accepted for registration with the United Kennel Club and the Field Dog Stud Book.

SUMMARY

AMERICAN WATER SPANIEL	(From working field stock.)
TYPE	Flushing breed-retriever.
WEIGHT	25 to 40 pounds.
HEIGHT AT WITHERS	15 to 18 inches.
COAT TYPE	Medium long, curly or waved and very dense; slightly oily.
COLOR	Solid liver or dark chocolate.
TAIL	Full length, covered with curly feathering.
MATURITY	16 to 18 months.

DISPOSITION	Gentle and affectionate with those he knows well; spaniellike in sensitivity; makes good house pet.
GAME BIRD SPECIALTIES	Good on ring-necked pheasant, also on woodcock and ruffed grouse; limited value on bobwhite quail and most other covey birds, except for fetching purposes (shooting preserve pheasants, chukar partridges, and single quail).
HUNTING RANGE	All flushing breeds must be trained to work within shotgun range, generally flushing quarry under 30 yards but never more than 40 from the gun.
TRAINABILITY RATING	Alert, intelligent, quick to learn, if handled with gentle firmness; sensitive as most spaniels, responds negatively to undue force or pressure.
OTHER REMARKS	Works at more methodical though merry pace than springer spaniel; good for hunters who prefer slower dog; very versatile breed that also hunts snipe, sora, and clapper rails, springs bunnies and makes good retriever for small water duck hunter; coat tends to pick up burrs and other debris.

CHAPTER 4

ON
BUYING
YOUR
PROSPECT

If you've followed the advice offered in the first chapter and carefully formulated all your requirements for the right type and breed of bird dog, and then gone on through the ten prime candidates in Chapters 2 and 3, the chances are excellent that you've now reached your decision. Having done so, you'll suddenly realize—if you're typical of most sportsmen about to buy their first bird dog—that you haven't the foggiest notion of where to locate the breed you want.

Your first thought will be the neighborhood pet shop—not necessarily an illogical idea, since pet shops sell puppies. The only trouble is they usually don't handle too many sporting breeds and those they do stock are virtually guaranteed to be two-thirds or more show breeding, generally pups suitable neither for the bench nor the field, but strictly house pet prospects. What to do?

Obtaining a few copies of the principal monthly hunting and fishing magazines and scanning their classified ads offers a good beginning toward locating several suitable sources of supply of the breed desired. Another logical possibility is your local newspaper, preferably a daily publication, although weeklies can also prove valuable for nearby sources listed in the classified sections.

The best approach may be a talk with your local sporting goods dealer—a man who usually has an intimate knowledge of everything pertaining to hunting, shooting, and angling within a 50- to 75-mile radius of his shop. A chat with your local game warden—someone it wouldn't hurt to know, anyway—can sometimes provide a solid lead on a local kennel or breeder who has a few pups of the breed you're looking for.

The outdoors editor of your local daily or weekly newspaper, or even of the nearest big metropolitan daily, is worth writing to or phoning, since he can often steer you to a reliable breeder. And, just as frequently, a local or regional commercial shooting preserve operator may either have or know of available pups of the breed you're seeking.

In addition, you always have recourse to the club secretary of the breed of your choice. Such officers are generally elected for multi-year terms and their names and addresses can be obtained by mail from the American Kennel Club. Ordinarily, writing to the breed club secretary, and enclosing a stamped, self-addressed envelope, will bring you a roster of area breeders who specialize in selling puppies of the breed of your choice.

In all probability, you won't know which of the sources will provide you with the best pup. The criteria normally involved in deciding are: reliability and integrity of the supplier; specific bloodlines desired or available; number of puppies from which to select; and price—pretty much in that order.

Checking on the reputability of a commercial breeder or kennel owner is simple enough: merely write to him and ask that he send you three references. Simultaneously, you can obtain all other pertinent information about the breeding, age, sex, and price of the puppies he currently has available.

Establishing the reliability of a private individual who offers puppies for sale is, of course, somewhat more difficult. Usually such persons are amateur breeders whose credentials may be open to question, although, as with any business transaction, requesting at least one business and one personal reference would hardly be out of

---

Above:
Gobs of affection and personal attention are the principal ingredients young puppies thrive on. Forget looking for bargain prices, though.
Photo by Robert Elman.
Below:
Mail-order puppies can be perfectly satisfactory, but buying a pup is such a personal thing that a visit to the kennel of your choice, where you can see the pups as well as the dam, is suggested procedure.

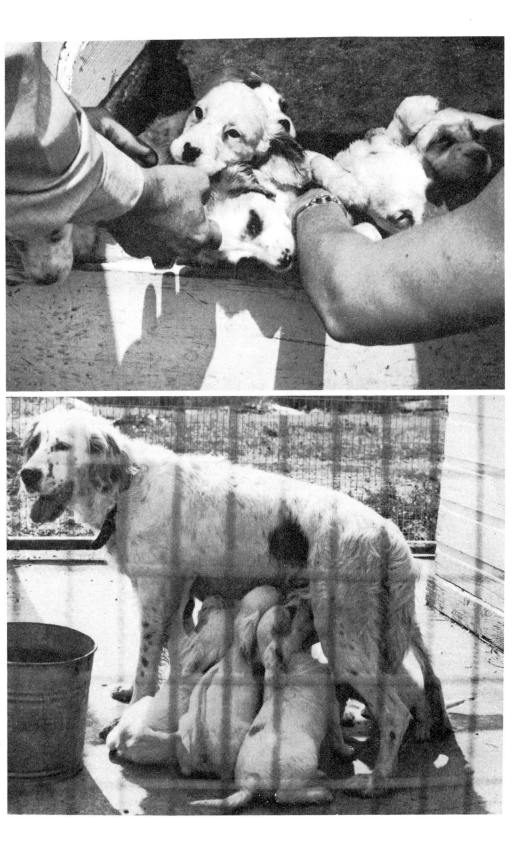

order. If the pups offered are a first litter, you will have no way of knowing how good or how poor they will turn out. However, if they are a second or even third litter out of the bitch in question, it is often possible to check with one or two buyers of puppies from previous litters to ascertain how well those pups are doing in the field.

Some experienced dog buyers avoid patronizing large commercial kennels in the belief that such establishments, having limited time and help, cannot give puppies the gobs of affection and personal attention they thrive upon. Numerous other buyers of varying degrees of experience are generally leery of ''home-bred litters'' unless the breeders and the litter's parents are known to them. Obviously, the question has its pros and cons.

There can be no getting away from the fact that the puppies most played with are environmentally advantaged over those that are merely fed and watered daily. Yet, if purchased shortly after being weaned—ordinarily between five and seven weeks of age—the puppy will readily imprint on his new owners. Therefore, even pups purchased from a large commercial kennel at an early age should not have suffered any undue disadvantages; nor should they have acquired any incurable faults.

Consideration of specific bloodlines is a subject you're going to have to get into totally, or not at all. The importance of good bloodlines in the bird dog cannot be stressed strongly enough. What constitutes good ancestry, however, is a question open to debate among even the most experienced dog men. There is a school of thought that disdains all field trial blood closer than four or five generations back in a puppy's pedigree. Another prefers as many field trial winners and champions as close up as possible. Still a third believes a reasonable mixture of celebrated and unheralded bloodlines offers the best potentiality. Who is right? That, of course, depends on who is talking at any given moment.

If we were considering field trial potential in a puppy that was to be campaigned seriously and used little as a gun dog, then there could be no question that a pedigree filled with field trial champions for four or five generations would offer the most likely candidate. However, since we are not looking for field trial prospects, but, rather, for dogs to be trained and used primarily as serviceable bird dogs, the above bloodlines might be considered too ''hot'' for the average amateur trainer to handle.

Yet, unless the buyer personally has knowledge of a pup's sire and dam, and even of their sires and dams, it is awfully difficult to project how well that puppy will measure up in the hunting field. That is where ancestry of some renown, such as field trial winners—not necessarily champions—provides a barometer for the buyer. Field trial winners are a matter of record and if their predecessors also were winners, it proves that their abilities in the field were passed along, in some degree, to their progeny.

Thus, if given a choice between a puppy from a line of uncelebrated ancestors and one from a line that contained at least a couple or three field trial winners within the previous two generations, this buyer would opt for the latter.

Whether you decide to deal with a large or small kennel or a private, amateur breeder will determine the number of litters and/or pups available for your selection. It goes without saying that the average private individual will usually have but a single litter for sale. The small professional breeder or kennel will seldom have more than one or two litters to choose from, and the large kennel may offer as many as three or four different litters for sale simultaneously.

The price you pay for your puppy should be the last consideration in your calculations. No reputable breeder, professional or amateur, of working bird dogs is likely to be guilty of price-gouging. It is not cheap to breed and properly raise a litter of puppies. The cost of maintaining good, healthy breeding stock has risen dramatically in recent years and, obviously, these increases must be reflected in the prices breeders ask for their puppies. Bargain pups seldom live up to that tag in later months and years. Besides, the initial investment you make in your puppy will prove to be inconsequential when prorated over a life span of ten, twelve, or even fourteen years of loyalty, service, and devotion.

Having winnowed the potential sources on the basis of the aforementioned criteria, your final choice will generally nominate itself by being close to home. Buying a puppy, especially your first bird dog, is too exciting an event to conclude by mail order. Not that there is anything necessarily wrong with purchasing a dog via mail and telephone; thousands are sold that way annually. But a puppy is such a personal thing that it should be selected personally by the prospective owner rather than picked out by the breeder and stuck in a shipping crate, to be subjected to all the rigors and possible hazards of long-distance travel.

Before you go anywhere near the kennel from which you intend to buy your puppy, you'll have several more decisions to make. Serious consideration must be given to your prospective pup's sex and age, along with the question of when (what time of year) you wish to make your purchase.

Most first dog buyers unhesitatingly want a male puppy, not so much because they really want a male, but, rather, because they are convinced they don't want a female. Females, more properly called bitches, come into heat and, if they get loose at the wrong time, can attract neighborhood swains by the dozen. Afterwards, a litter of unwanted mongrel pups can be difficult to sell or even give away. Since bitches usually are less expensive than dogs (males), the average buyer surmises that they must be inferior.

Certainly, it is a biological fact that bitches do experience three-week heat periods twice annually and must be closely restricted during those times. But, unless it would create an undue problem to keep her relegated to the kitchen or a fenced-in backyard kennel at such times, there is no reason why a buyer should not give equal consideration to choosing a bitch puppy. In fact, solid arguments could be cited for the first dog buyer to favor getting a bitch rather than a dog.

For one thing, a bitch is normally more docile than a dog, hence, more submissive to control. She is also more dependent upon and affectionate toward her master, qualities that generally make a bitch a bit more responsive to training. Additionally, most bitches are smaller and weigh less than their male counterparts, a conceivably significant advantage in less than spacious quarters. These are some of the advantageous qualities of the female canine with which the uninitiated buyer may not be acquainted.

How old a puppy should you look for? Should it be five-to-seven weeks, eight-to-twelve weeks, three-to-five months of age, or older? During the past two decades a good deal of scientific study of canines has been conducted and given considerable publicity by various authors. In brief, the research deals with a timetable of canine mental development and advises purchase of a puppy at a precise age—the study says that the younger the puppy, after reaching his seventh week, the more pliable he'll be, and therefore, the more susceptible

---

Above:
Know what you want, as to the age and sex of a puppy, before you get to the kennel or other place of purchase. Once you arrive you'll face decisions enough in trying to make a choice. Photo by Robert Elman.

Below:
Play with the pups in the litter of your choice. Observe their responses to your presence, movements, conversation, noises, as well as their interaction with one another. Photo by Robert Elman.

he'll be to accepting training. Of course, long before such research was undertaken, many people had been buying weanling pups in the firm conviction that the younger a pup could be introduced to his new home and surroundings, the more easily his personality could be molded.

While there are advantages to obtaining a weanling puppy, there also are disadvantages. The younger the puppy, the higher the risk of his contracting serious diseases. Very young pups, having little control of their tiny bladders and bowels, present more difficulties in house-breaking, and even when fairly well confined can be unbelievably destructive in their playfulness. Toddlers and very young puppies don't mix well either. A six- or seven-week old pup, though he may seem pretty rugged, is seldom able to withstand the constant mauling of a persistent three-year-old child.

Older pups, say from about three to four months of age, eliminate some of these hazards and minimize others. At the same time, they offer the buyer a better idea about their potentialities, in terms of markings, coloration, and temperament, while still being young enough to successfully adapt to a new environment and a different owner.

Overall, we'd advise obtaining a puppy as young as feasible for your particular situation and circumstances.

As mentioned earlier, an important consideration is when to purchase your puppy. Obviously, there are certain times of year that are more advantageous than others. The ideal time to raise a litter of pups is during the spring, just as the weather begins to warm.

Breeders, both amateur and professional, being well aware of this, time their litters to coincide as closely as possible with mild weather rearing conditions. Generally, this means that puppies whelped in March through May will be weaned and available for purchase between mid-April and early July. Obviously, with the laws of supply and demand in force, these are the best months in which to buy your pup. Later, with fewer and older pups left over, you'll not only have less of a selection but may also have to pay a higher price.

When you are ready to pick out your bird dog pup, make an appointment with the breeder so he'll be expecting you and can allot the time you need. Take your wife along, but leave the kids at home. The fewer opinions, especially the nonobjective kind, injected into selecting a good puppy, the less complex will be your decision-making process. Besides, the kids will love whichever pup you bring home.

100   Your moment of truth is when you are at the breeder's establish-

ment, faced by anywhere from five to eight of the cutest bundles of fur, flailing tails, flapping ears, bouncy feet, and soulful eyes you've ever seen. But how do you narrow down your choice to the best pup in the litter? Before you even start trying, dismiss the idea that there is a "best" pup in any litter. It's a relative matter, really. What you should be looking for is a good, healthy puppy, one that displays no significant defects and that seems most typical of the breed. He or she should be friendly and curious, though not necessarily effusive.

Eliminate from contention immediately the pup that shuns any physical contact with you, shying away from your touch and shrinking nervously in the far corner of his kennel run. Feel sorry for him if you must, but don't let your emotions—or those of your wife—influence your objectivity.

Although not always a sure sign of ultimate size, both the smallest and the largest puppies in a litter should be eliminated from consideration. After all, you don't want either a giant or a midget and it's better to avoid as many risks as possible.

After you've played with the puppies for a few minutes, all the while observing and making mental note of their responses to your presence, movements, conversation, and noises, as well as of their interaction with one another, leave them. Try to observe the pups from a place of concealment. This small act of espionage can prove as revealing as it usually is entertaining, providing you an even better insight into how the puppies get along together and amuse themselves when alone.

By this time you've probably reduced your candidates to two or three dogs or bitches, depending upon which sex you want. Now is the time to ask the breeder to let you see these tentative choices, each separately, out in the yard or in another room away from the security of their kin and kennel. In unfamiliar environs, each puppy will be on his own, reflecting his true character and personality. The puppy most desirable will evidence boldness combined with an inquisitive, investigative nature.

Be alert not to mistake boldness for thickheadedness or reasonable cautiousness for timidity. If a pup were to paw the prongs of an upturned rake and squeal in discomfort, then immediately repeat the act, that would be cause to suspect thickheadedness. However, having hurt himself the first time, if he approached the rake again, this time slowly, carefully, and gave the prongs a thorough sniffing, that could be construed as boldness, tempered with justifiable caution.

There are other more formal regimen—again the result of animal behaviorists' research—designed to select pups with the most or

Above, left:
Watch the pups unbeknownst to them, if possible. Take special note of how the ones you're interested in get along with their litter mates. Photo by Robert Elman.

Above, top right:
Take your two or three tentative selections, each separately, out in the yard, away from the security of their kin and kennel. Photo by Robert Elman.

Above, bottom right:
Pointing breed pups, such as this six-week-old English setter, can be checked for curiosity and pointing instinct by moving a bird wing along the ground in front of them. Photo by Robert Elman.

*In unfamiliar environs, each puppy will be strictly on his own,
revealing his true character and personality, boldly investigating
strange objects or shrinking away from them.*

least submissive dispositions and varying degrees in between.
Perhaps these methods have a great deal of merit or very little; never
having tried them ourselves, we truthfully do not know. Since they
seem a bit too formularized, as well as time consuming, and the
means by which we have always chosen pups has seldom disap-
pointed us, there seems little point in adopting such techniques.

Having thoroughly checked out your two or three prospects, you
should have been able to finalize your choice. Should there be any   103

gnawing doubts in your mind, don't hesitate to discuss them openly with the breeder and ask for his advice. Naturally, he'll want you to be completely satisfied and happy with the puppy you take home; his advice will be given accordingly and, certainly, can be accepted as sincere.

Along with the breeder you should double check the pup for any physical defects you might have missed seeing earlier. His eyes should be bright and clear and show no signs of discharging matter. His ears should look and smell clean, indicating that they, too, are free from discharge, infection, or parasites. The pup's nose should be cool and just slightly moist, although a warm, dry nose is not necessarily indicative of any serious problems. His teeth and mouth should be clean and free from any offensive odor. Check his gums, which should be healthfully pink; a palish white hue usually means anemia, generally caused by parasitic infestation.

Aside from the above precautions, don't worry too much about the health of the pup you pick. One of the conditions of sale should be that your own veterinarian will examine the pup within 48 to 72 hours and give him a clean bill of health. Should the breeder object to your returning the pup for refund or replacement if your vet finds him in ill health, simply walk away from the deal. No reputable breeder will disclaim responsibility for the health of one of his pups if examined and disapproved by a licensed veterinarian, within reasonable time—usually ten days—after purchase.

The breeder should provide you with details of the puppy's health record: shots (the kind and brand name, if possible; dates); worming (dates and for what kinds of worms; whether done by microscopic examination by a vet or on pure guesswork by the breeder; or if not wormed at all); feed (what brand and type; quantity and number of daily feedings). In addition, you should obtain the necessary papers—all properly signed and dated—with which you can register your pup in the same kennel club stud book in which his forebears were registered.

Above:
After checking with the breeder on all pertinent data concerning the pup's care, feeding, and medical record, you can close the deal and start for home. Photo by Robert Elman.
Below:
Safely ensconced in a corrugated box, lined with a thick layer of newspapers, your new puppy will doubtless begin a permanent love affair with the better half.

Oftentimes, a breeder will own the bitch who is mother to the pups, but not own the sire, in which case he may not yet have obtained signed certificates of the date of service from the owner of the sire. If the breeder is reputable—and you should already have determined that he is—there is no need to insist on obtaining this document on the spot. You can generally rely on the breeder's promise to mail it to you as soon as possible.

When you've closed the deal, after making sure to double check all pertinent data concerning the puppy's regular care and feeding and bought a four or five day supply of chow from the breeder, all that remains is to safely transport your new acquisition home. Doubtless you will have made some provision for keeping the puppy confined during the trip home. A corrugated box, open at the top and containing a thick layer of newspapers on the bottom, makes a very handy carrier for puppies under eight or nine weeks old.

For an older puppy, who is apt to be more rambunctious and capable of making considerably greater mess, a carrying crate of wire or aluminum serves as the best, safest, and most comfortable means of transporting him. Since such a crate is virtually a must for all future car trips with your pup, it constitutes a wise investment prior to your pup's actual purchase. Remember, though, to choose a crate large enough to accommodate your pup when he reaches his full size at maturity.

As you leave the kennel with that new little devil safely ensconced in the car, don't forget to keep your eyes on the road and your mind on your driving. There'll be plenty of time for you to get acquainted—the rest of his life, in fact—once you arrive home.

CHAPTER 5

YOUR PUP'S EARLY HOME LIFE

For several weeks before selecting your puppy, you should have been busy making preparations for his or her arrival. If you've done your homework, everything will go a lot more smoothly during those first several days—and nights.

First, you should have purchased a few of the essential supplies you'll need, such as a suitable metal or high-impact plastic food and water bowl, a decent quality leash and collar (bear in mind the age of the pup and the fact that he'll grow out of a tiny collar very quickly), a comb, brush, some nail clippers, a can of spray deodorizer, and some sort of rawhide bone to ease the eventual discomfort of his teething and also to keep him occupied.

Of course, you will have determined where he'll sleep and in or on what. Remember that car crate mentioned in the previous chapter? It also serves as an excellent dog bed and does double duty by keeping the pup confined during the night and at certain times of the day. Since most puppies do not like to soil the place where they sleep, the crate generally aids in the housebreaking process, too. A layer of newspapers lining the bottom of the crate will serve as a bed and can be changed when and if the need arises.

Where his bed will be is a matter of preference and convenience, but 99 times out of 100 the kitchen will get the nod. Wherever you choose to have him sleep, however, make certain it is warm and free from drafts.

Ideally, you will have arrived home with the pup as early in the day as possible. This will permit him lots of time to familiarize himself with his new surroundings before bedtime and just might give you and the family a better chance of enjoying some sleep, something likely to be a scarce commodity for three or four nights.

After allowing him his preliminary scouting foray—and you should know you're taking considerable risk if you permit him to explore the whole house—the pup can be given a small bowl of slightly warm milk. Two or three tablespoons of corn flakes, Wheaties, or even the kibble supplied by the breeder may be added, but in no event should he be fed a large meal prior to his first night in his new home.

By all means, play with him; do not attempt to correct or punish him, or holler or speak abnormally loudly to him. Give him virtually free rein; let him become familiar with and confident about his new home and owners. When you put him to bed that night, several ploys can be tried to ascertain that he'll accept his new surroundings and the absence of mom and litter mates with reasonable grace.

A loud ticking clock, such as the old-fashioned wind-up type, sometimes keeps a pup from feeling too lonesome, and its monotonous metronomic effect often lulls him quickly to sleep. A radio, tuned softly to one of those all-night talk shows, frequently has the same effect. The warmth of a hot water bottle, reminiscent as it is of the body heat of the pup's dam or litter mates, also will sometimes suffice to provide the security needed to induce sleep.

During those first few weeks in his new environment, the puppy will be absorbing a great deal of knowledge, whether you deliberately try to teach him or not. Naturally, it's important that what he picks up by osmosis be restricted, as much as possible, to proper, normal behavior and good habits.

Among the good habits you must teach him is one of the most

Above:
Since the collar is something your pup has to get used to sooner or later, it should be placed on him soon after he's scouted out his new home.
Below:
Make friends and play with him as soon as possible. Don't try to correct or punish him. Let him become familiar with and confident about his new home and owners.

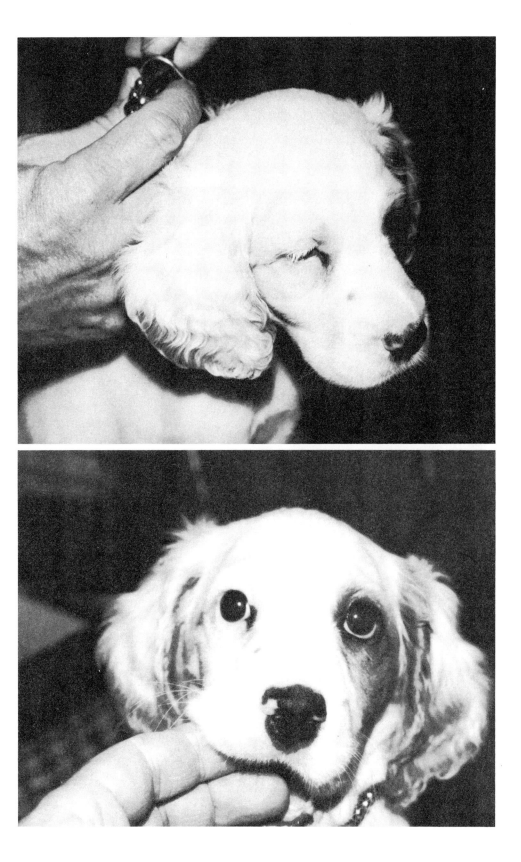

important immediate things he'll need to learn—to become housebroken. Either of two basic approaches can be used. *Paperbreaking* is easier and has some advantages over the *direct* system of housebreaking. It is usually preferred for training young puppies—six to eight weeks old—whose bladders and bowels move frequently, and where owners must be absent from the house for extended periods.

Essentially, it encourages the puppy to relieve himself only where newspapers are spread, starting initially with a fairly large area of the room and eventually limiting it to a very small section. Whenever the pup eats or drinks, or right after he wakes from a nap, he should be placed on the papers at the first indications of restlessness. When he relieves himself on the papers, you must praise him; when he goes elsewhere, you must catch him in the act and immediately scold him. If you can catch him just before he errs, place him on the newspapered section and, as he completes his "job," let him know you think he's a really good dog.

The direct system for housebreaking, although far more tedious for master or mistress, is the one we personally prefer. It is based on rigid routine and constant vigilance, requiring an unvarying feeding and outdoor exercise regimen. As in paperbreaking, you must be alert to the very first signs of restiveness in the puppy after he eats, drinks, exercises, or wakes up. Taking him out immediately to a single small area in the yard is the only formula for success. Keep him out until he performs the necessary functions, at which time you should lavish him with vocal praise and a pat on the head.

Ordinarily, housebreaking a normal, healthy puppy is not a difficult task; the only requirements are consistency, patience, and time. The younger the pup, the more time it will take, but there is no logical reason for not beginning his housebreaking training routine as soon as he arrives in your home.

Proper feeding of your puppy is, of course, part of the care you must give him continuously from the moment you bring him home and he becomes your responsibility. Most pups require feeding about three times a day, up to the age of six months. From six months to about one year, twice daily feedings are recommended. After reaching his first birthday, one meal a day should suffice.

What to feed your pup will depend on a number of aspects: what his breeder was feeding, what your veterinarian recommends, and your own pocketbook. Generally, your choice of foods will include canned meat (some combining cereal filler), dry meal or kibble, or the newer soft-moist types. Regardless of which type you ultimately decide to use, your pup should be given measured amounts so that

Left:
If you've wisely chosen a bold puppy, he'll display his independence
and spirit in obvious ways, though not necessarily by climbing up the
front of a Kennel-Aire crate.
Right:
Proper feeding of your pup is one of the most vital aspects of his
daily care. To help in housebreaking him, feed him at regular
intervals each day and take him out on schedule.

you'll be able to regulate his portions according to his specific needs, growth rates, and condition.

He should be fed at the same times each day so that he and you can become familiarized with a regular routine, something that, as already mentioned, will aid immensely in teaching him indoor cleanliness. The hours you select should be those that will be most convenient for you and/or your wife. Obviously, if dealing with a puppy under six months old that requires three feedings daily, you would space them more or less around your own breakfast, lunch, and dinner hours. Don't forget, though, that the young puppy must be taken out, usually within fifteen to thirty minutes after eating; so don't feed him just as you're ready to sit down to your own meal. III

Everything we've pointed out thus far has been on the assumption that your puppy will share your home with you, rather than be kenneled outdoors. Even if your pup will live in a backyard kennel, it's still a good idea to let him spend some time in the house, especially during the initial weeks after leaving his dam and kennel mates. Throughout his life, he should be permitted in the house on a fairly regular basis to give him a greater sense of belonging.

In general, aside from his needing more and more of your time and attention as he grows toward maturity, caring for a young dog is not a complex chore. He will require some grooming, daily exercise, and periodic checkups by the veterinarian, who will advise you when to bring him in for whatever additional innoculations and wormings he'll require.

The word grooming can sometimes scare people, conjuring up visions of complicated barbering and special clips such as are normally associated with poodles. As far as grooming most hunting breeds goes, it seldom involves much more than trimming nails when they grow too long, a daily or thrice weekly brushing and combing, and an occasional bath. Some breeds need to have their coats trimmed a bit with electric clippers, but such haircuts usually are necessary only two or three times a year.

Daily exercise is a necessity for a bird dog, right from his puppyhood through his waning years. Some of this exercise can be combined with the regular outings during which he relieves himself. An extra trip or two outdoors for a short romp in the yard, however, should be included in his schedule every day, the only exceptions being caused by inclement weather or emergencies.

Along with his regular routine care, feeding, and housebreaking, your pup should begin learning some of the niceties of becoming "civilized." Part of this process will stem from the fact that he has a name and therefore an identity. Whatever registration name you ultimately decide upon is unimportant compared with the everyday or call name you give him. This should be a one or two syllable name—the shorter, the better—easy to pronounce, easy for him to recognize, and with a distinctive sound unlike any of the commands you will use in his training.

All the commands necessary to train your bird dog will be discussed in detail later; they are listed here so you will not make the mistake of choosing a name with any similarity to them:

NO...HERE...SIT...HUP...WHOA...HEEL...DOWN...
STAY...GO ON...DEAD...FETCH...HOLD...GIVE...
ALL RIGHT...KENNEL...CLO-O-O-SE...BACK...OVER...

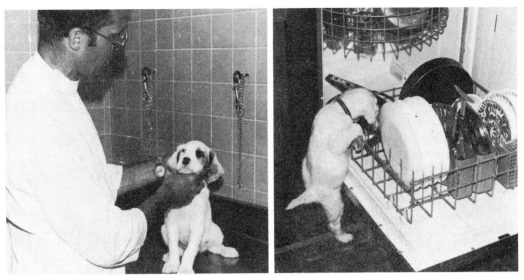

Left:
It's important to take your pup to your local veterinarian for a complete checkup within 48 to 72 hours after you bring him home. Your veterinarian can advise you of future shots and wormings at that time.
Right:
Part of your pup's becoming "civilized" is getting used to the everyday routine of your household. The noise of pots and pans clanging in the kitchen will help condition him. You should guard against his overexuberance, however.

You should select a call name for your pup as soon as, or even before, you buy and bring him home. Use it whenever you speak to him. You'll be pleasantly surprised at how quickly even a very young pup learns his name and visibly responds to it. As we said, it gives him an identity and it also serves you by getting his attention prior to your issuing a command.

For the first couple of months, most of your pup's rudimentary education will be gained simply through exposure to all the things that make up his environment. The whole world is new to him; everything is interesting and should be investigated. Encourage his curiosity and let him experience as many new sights, sounds, and smells as possible. He'll profit greatly from such exposure.

During this time, you'll have to provide the guidance he'll need in 113 order to develop into a properly civilized dog. He should be familiarized with the basic commands—No, Here, Sit, Hup, Stay, and All Right—as soon as he has shown that he's accepted and trusts you and is no longer a stranger to his new surroundings. Usually, that means that such instruction can begin within three or four days after his arrival. (All of the step-by-step details of teaching these commands will be found in Chapter 7.)

Remember that your puppy is still just a baby and has to be dealt with gently and patiently. Never forget, either, that you are teaching, not overpowering your pupil. Don't permit impatience to heat up your cool: an angry trainer always loses—at least the battle and sometimes the war.

Punishment, this early in the game, should be limited to vocal chastisement, a displeased or shaming tone of voice normally sufficing to get your point across. When your pup starts demonstrating that he understands what you are asking him to do, by actually doing it, let him know how much he's pleased you. Make a fuss over him, pet him, tell him he's the greatest dog in the world. Then repeat the command that he just obeyed. The chances are good that he will again comply. If so, make another fuss over him; he'll know he's pleasing you and he'll enjoy the fact.

Getting used to a collar and leash is something your pup must do sooner or later. Actually, the collar should be placed on a new puppy after he's been in the house only a few hours, and should remain on him continuously. It should be just tight enough for you to slip two fingers under comfortably. He will be aware of it immediately and begin trying to scratch it off. Let him try briefly, then start playing with him, to divert his attention from the collar. Each time he remembers that it's there, he'll sit down and start scratching; and each time, you should attempt to distract him. Soon, the intervals between his scratching will increase and in no time at all he'll forget about the collar entirely.

Becoming accustomed to the leash is usually a lot more difficult for a puppy. There are two methods by which it can be accomplished. The first is a gradual process that calls for attaching a yard-long lightweight rope to his collar, letting him drag it around and playing with it whenever he wishes.

During the four or five days that he's got the rope tagging along

---

When you first put the leash on him, he'll rebel, rearing and bucking, just like a wild bronco, but eventually accepting the fact that the restraint doesn't really do him any harm.

wherever he goes, you should occasionally grab the end of it. Never jerk it sharply; simply let the pup know, by exerting slight pressure on it, that you are in a position to restrain him. He won't like that and will tug vigorously against the rope until you eventually let it go. Within a few days, he'll begin to accept the fact that your hanging onto the rope doesn't really do him any harm. After that, all you have to do is get him used to walking with you on the rope, for which you'll soon substitute the regular leash you've bought for him.

The second method—the one we personally prefer—does away with the long, drawn-out procedure above and gets right to the heart of the matter. It involves attaching a lightweight leash to the pup's collar and letting him discover one of the hard facts of life right away. When he first feels the restraint of the leash, he'll dance at the end of it like a bucking bronco. Permit him to fight it for about ten seconds and then take the pressure off, giving him enough slack so that all he feels is the weight of the leash.

Let him lead you around for a couple of minutes before you tighten up on the leash again. Doubtless, the same wild gyrations will ensue, but this time make him fight the leash a little longer before you slacken it. Do this for about ten minutes, three or four times a day, and your pup should be well broken to the leash within three days, about three times faster than the first method described can accomplish the job.

At first opportunity after you've gotten your new puppy acclimated to the house, to you and your family and your regular daily routine, you should begin car-breaking him. Sure, he rode home from the kennel with you and then down to your veterinarian and back a couple of days later. But that hardly means he's car-broken. Besides, he probably got car sick at least once on each occasion.

Since your bird dog and your car must eventually become well acquainted, it makes good sense to establish in the pup the proper attitude toward the family buggy. Initially, even though he has had a couple of rides, the best means of indoctrination is to let your pup spend a few minutes every day just sitting with you in the parked car and exploring its interior. Talking to him in normal tones and encouraging him to play and explore will assure him that the car is not a bad place to be.

After four or five days of such exercise, start the engine and let the pup become accustomed to the sound of it idling. If the noise doesn't seem to bother him, repeat the procedure one more day, just for insurance. Then, the next time, take a short ride—around the block is about right for openers—to condition him to the car's motion. If

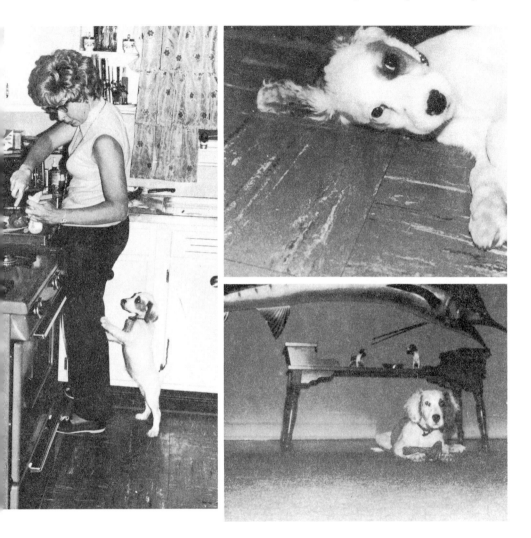

Left:
If he's normal, your puppy should adapt quickly to his new environment. Don't shield him from routine events. When he's a bit older and more trustworthy, let him spend more time with you, to build greater rapport.
Top right:
After his playtime, let him rest. Young puppies need lots of sleep.
Bottom right:
Ignore him when he shies from something.

117

possible, drive him around the block two or three separate times that day and for the next two or three days.

Try to take your drives with the pup as long after his most recent feeding as you can, to diminish the chances of his getting car sick. This precaution, in combination with brief but frequent drives, should enable you to gradually lengthen the trips after a week or so, with the pup showing no signs of fear, unease, or motion sickness. Once he arrives at this stage, start putting him in his carrying crate in the car whenever you take a drive. For safety's sake, your dog should always be crated while traveling in an automobile.

With the exception of familiarizing your puppy with the basic commands mentioned earlier, to make your job of serious training easier later on, most of what he learns during his early home life will be, in simplest terms, to adjust satisfactorily. Or, as we stated earlier, to become civilized. As noted, a young puppy is quick to pick up habits, good and bad. The most important job at this stage will be to help create and maintain the proper atmosphere in which your pup begins growing up.

He should not be shielded unduly from the normal routine of his new home; after all, he has to become accustomed to the clatter of pots and pans, the vacuum cleaner, the TV set, the shouts and laughter of kids at play. But neither should he be subjected to teasing by something that frightens him. Children of any age must be cautioned about teasing or playing too roughly with a young puppy, and should be supervised for a while to make certain they comply with parental instructions.

Eventually, children old enough to do so should be permitted to participate in some of the day-to-day care of the new puppy. They can help brush and comb and exercise him. These things, combined with affectionate play, will give the pup a greater sense of belonging and security, as well as help build a closer dog-human relationship.

This dog-human relationship, rapport, companionship, by whatever name you choose to identify it, is one of the most vital aspects of your pup's early home life and is the very foundation on which all of his future training rests. If your rapport is strong and your mutual affection great, your puppy will, because of his more intense eagerness to please, become far more receptive to learning everything else you must teach him in the future.

PRELIMINARY FIELD TRIPS

After your pup's been at home for about two or three weeks, you can begin taking him afield. Assuming he's between eight and eleven weeks old, he will not be too young to enjoy and benefit from an early introduction to the big outdoors.

Presumably, too, you will have followed our advice and purchased your pup sometime between mid-April and early July. If so, then by the time you take him afield, the weather will be pleasantly warm. Obviously, if you bought your pup very late or very early in the year, you'll have to put off his field outings until snow and cold weather have disappeared.

Just as the basic commands you've begun to familiarize him with have been informally introduced, so, too, should his preliminary field trips be kept casual. They are opportunities for him to become acquainted with as many of the objects that make up the outdoor world as possible. And, at the tender age of two or three months, his curiosity will be inexhaustible, once he begins getting over his apprehension about straying too far from your side.

His first half-dozen or so outings need not be longer than fifteen or twenty minutes duration. Preferably, they should be on consecutive days, but that, of course, is not always possible. If you can arrange to get him out on weekends and at least once during the week, so much the better.

Try, also, to vary the locations where you can run your pup, so he doesn't become used to just one place and one type of terrain and cover. Be sure to keep him out of any hazardous areas, such as heavy quagmires, precipitous hill country, or places dotted with deep sinkholes, while he's still physically immature.

Essentially, these first few trips afield should condition the very young pup to a wide variety of things he will always encounter outdoors. Let him take the time to check out anything that entices or intrigues him—fluttering leaves, grasshoppers, butterflies, frogs, stones, whatever is new and different. If something backs him off,

---

Opposite, above:
An occasional rest period during your short outings permits you to play with your pup, letting him know the association between you extends outside the house.
Opposite, below:
An early introduction to the great outdoors will benefit your pup, giving him a chance to explore and investigate.
Below:
All sorts of strange new sights and smells that captivate his curiosity will overcome any reticence about leaving your side, at least for a couple of minutes at a time.

give him the opportunity, and some encouragement, to reinvestigate and allay his fear of it.

If your pup shows considerable hesitancy to leave your side during the first couple of walks afield, don't fret too much about it. He's still very young and, obviously, a bit insecure. However, unless he proves to be the rare exception among bird dog breeds, sooner or later he'll find something that will attract his interest and move him out ahead of you. Once he gains a bit more self-confidence, his curiosity will continue to overcome his early reticence to explore.

Most average bird dog puppies, regardless of type or breed, will quickly become accustomed to running about in the field or woods. At only two or three months of age, they will still be awkward and slow enough for you not only to keep tabs on but to catch, if necessary. You should not, however, attempt to exercise any formal or obvious control over your pup during his initial field indoctrination. Simply because he is very young, and everything in the big outdoor world is new, he'll want to keep apprised of your whereabouts and will continually check to see that you're still nearby. This is one of the big pluses of introducing him to the field early, promoting in him the habit of keeping track of you, something that will stand you in good stead later on when you're hunting him.

After five or six outings, your pup will probably have lost all or most of his strangeness in the outdoors. Even though his physical immaturity will restrict him, you should be able to detect a greater eagerness in his attitude, a perceptible increase in his desire to romp and explore. As you notice this taking place, you should begin doing a few things that will slowly condition the pup toward developing a hunting pattern in his movement through the field.

Whenever you unleash him in the field, tell him "Go On," and at the same time blow two short toots on your whistle. This is the conventionally used signal to start a dog hunting and to get him moving again after he's stopped, for whatever reason. Certainly it won't mean anything to your puppy at first. Soon, however, he'll learn that the double toot is a welcome sound that tells him he can run free. Later, after it has become an ingrained response, your signal will serve in a variety of ways, to be discussed in detail later.

While your pup is romping freely, adopt a course that will keep him out in front of you as much of the time as possible. Whenever he changes direction, change your own so that he will always be to your front. He won't know your moves are deliberate, but eventually he'll come to realize that he's supposed to be out front, because you've conditioned him to believe it's only natural.

In time, when he's a little older, you should do the leading. In other words, you should set the course, and each time you turn, call the pup's name, wave your arm in the direction you want to go, and simultaneously blow two short blasts on your whistle. If he fails to turn, then you'll have to wait right where you are. Since he has become used to having you fairly close behind him, it shouldn't take him more than a couple of minutes to miss you and start hunting you up—perhaps even a bit apprehensively.

Counting on this, start moving slowly, splitting the difference in the angle between the general direction you had signaled and the one your pup took. It's a good bet your pup will backtrack and spot you not far from where you originally signaled your change of direction. As soon as you know he sees you, call his name and give him the arm and whistle signal to take the new course. You can almost make book on the fact that he'll comply this time. If he does, repeat the procedure once more, a few minutes later. However, if he doesn't, then forget your whistle and arm signaling for the rest of that outing.

All of this should be kept informal. It's an almost subliminal conditioning of the pup to the formal training that will follow. At this early age, your puppy should not receive any correction or discipline whatever while he's in the field.

How many times you can get him out in the field after his first several trips will depend on your own personal situation: how far from your house you must go to get to the field and whether you can run him mornings, evenings, or only on weekends. The more often you take him afield from the beginning, the more quickly he'll start behaving more instinctively like a hunting dog.

If you can take him out three or four days a week for a couple of months, he should be well acclimated to the outdoors by the time he's four or five months old. Remember, these trips need only be for about twenty minutes. Keeping him out much longer may either tire or bore him, and you don't want to risk doing that.

Since you'll be going afield with your pup during the summer months, check your local game regulations to make certain you can legally run a bird dog puppy at that time; and run him only during the cooler periods of the day, which means either early morning or late evening. Some states prohibit having a bird dog afield during the months when wild game birds are nesting and rearing their young. (Example: In New York State, dogs may be taken afield for training on wild game from August 1 to April 1 only.)

Assuming you're unhampered by any regulations against running your pup, he will certainly have bumped into at least a few song

Opposite, above:
By adopting a zigzag course and blowing two short whistle toots
everytime you change direction, you'll help your pup establish a
natural hunting pattern.
Opposite, below:
When your pup's emerging instincts have him enthusiastically
chasing birds, you can introduce the sound of gunfire.
Below:
If you can get the odd fresh-killed pigeon or small game bird and
encourage your puppy to play with and retrieve it, you'll stimulate
his interest in birds early.

birds, sparrows, and possibly even a game bird or two during his preliminary trips afield. If he's at least moderately bold, chances are the pup will begin chasing anything he flushes by about his third outing. This should be encouraged; talk to him in excited, but normally modulated tones, indicating that you, too, think his chasing birds is really great fun. He'll still be too young to chase very far, or to catch a bird, so you needn't worry about either aspect.

Whatever you do, don't make the mistake of coddling your puppy outdoors. When you come to some sort of obstacle, such as an old stone fence or very shallow brook, try to pick the easiest way across for him, without going too far out of your way. If he hesitates to follow, simply call his name and urge him on, then turn and continue on your way. He may whimper and scamper back and forth a bit, even trying to find another place to cross, but you should not relent and help him as long as he's in no danger and can physically negotiate the obstacle himself.

If he tries but backs off, the obstacle may actually be too tough for a pup his age to negotiate. If he absolutely refuses to try, he may just be a bit timid yet. In either case, don't let him suspect that you've noticed his failure. What you must do is casually change your direction—giving him the two-toot whistle signal and arm movement—to parallel the fence or brook for a short distance before crossing again to his side. Eventually, he'll start taking such obstacles right in stride.

You may be wondering when your puppy should be introduced to the sound of the gun, to avoid the problem of gunshyness. Some people contend that firing a cap pistol to signal feeding time should commence as soon as a pup is weaned. The theory is that the cap should first be popped about 50 feet away as chow is brought to the pup, gradually diminishing the distance over a period of two to three weeks. If the pup accepts the noise, the cap pistol is replaced by a .22 caliber blank and the regimen begun all over again. Finally, the pup graduates to hearing a .410 bore shotgun and, later, a 20 gauge.

This method, used mostly by professional trainers who can accustom a whole kennel full of dogs of all ages to gunfire, is effective—for them. It may be equally effective for you, too, if your pup is kenneled in the yard and you live in a rural area, where anything

---

Give your young dog as many opportunities as possible to go afield and find birds, but be careful not to rush his familiarization by pushing him into formal lessons before he's ready. Photo by Vern D. Brand.

126

louder than a cap gun going off several times a day won't find the neighbors siccing the town cops on you.

A second group believes, and we concur, that the field is the best place and time to introduce pointing breeds to the sound of gunfire, especially if your pup shares indoor quarters with you, since even cap guns, much less .22 blanks, going off would scare the wits out of everybody in the house, including the pup.

Spaniels and retrievers used as flushing dogs, however, can be introduced to the sound of the gun soon after their informal fetch training has produced reasonable regularity in their retrieving thrown dummies to hand. As a rule, you can expect to begin accustoming a flushing dog to the noise of a cap pistol by the time he's about four or five months old and move him up to .22 blanks within another month or two.

Concurrent with your young puppy's introduction to the big outdoors, you'll be conditioning him to retrieving. Since this is a strong natural instinct, it is one of the easiest informal lessons he can learn.

An old sock, handkerchief, or glove, knotted several times, makes an adequate "dummy" with which to start your pup fetching. These objects are light and small enough for a young puppy to pick up, and of a texture he'll enjoy carrying in his mouth. For these first informal fetch sessions, the locale is very important. A confined area indoors, free from any distractions, is ideal.

After letting the pup thoroughly investigate the area, tantalize him with your makeshift dummy. Skid it erratically around the floor, enticing him to pounce on and grab it. Don't let him catch it, but, when he's really excited about the object, slide it about 4 feet across the floor in front of him, using a slow, deliberate tossing motion.

As he rushes over and picks up the dummy, call his name and tell him "Fetch" in a crisp but happy tone, coaxing him to return to you with the object. From your kneeling or squatting position you may have to slap your thigh and add the word "Here" in order to cajole him into bringing you his prize. However, chances are he'll come right to you. Pet him profusely, all the while telling him what a fine pup he is as you take the sock, handkerchief, or glove from him.

Under no circumstances should you permit him to involve you in a game of tug of war with the object. If he grudgingly refuses to release it, slip your left hand under his lower jaw and squeeze his lips against his teeth. Normally, this firm but gentle pressure will make him open his mouth and release his hold on the object. As he does so, remove the article and command "Give." Follow up with lavish praise and petting, to let him know how pleased you are with him.

Run through the procedure four or five times, quitting while the pup's interest is still high. Make it part of your daily routine, if possible, but do it at least every other day. In fairly short order, you'll notice how eager your puppy becomes when he sees the sock, handkerchief, or glove in your hand. Keep each session brief, limiting the pup to no more than five or six "retrieves" at a time.

After half-a-dozen such sessions, try lobbing the dummy a foot or two farther. If the pup responds properly, continue tossing about the same distance for another week. A recalcitrant pup should not be reprimanded or punished in any way; simply withhold praise, shorten your throws, and begin all over again.

The progressive pup can start becoming conditioned to noise at this stage. Everytime you pitch the dummy, clap your hands just once and tell the pup to "Fetch." The sharp handclap will seldom bother a normal pup and it will serve, for a brief period, as the sound of the cap gun that will be introduced within a couple of weeks, or whenever you are convinced that its report will not upset or unnerve your pup.

During all of the informal fetch sessions with your spaniel or retriever puppy, you should never use the command "Fetch," or clap your hands, or fire a cap gun without actually tossing your makeshift dummy for him to retrieve. In addition to making a game of something he must be enthusiastic about doing—retrieving to hand—you are instilling in him the trust and confidence you want him to feel about his master, while simultaneously accustoming him to simulated gunfire. This multiple-purpose informal training is obviously beneficial to your entire program of future yard and field work when casual informality begins turning into serious and demanding business. (The flushing dog's fetch training will be discussed in detail in Chapter 11.)

Some of this informal fetch training to be used with the flushing breeds also has application to the pointing breeds. But since pointers do not take to fetching as instinctively and naturally as do the spaniels and retrievers, they are customarily force-trained to retrieve (a procedure that's fully explained in Chapter 10).

Pointing dogs should *never* be taught to retrieve—and certainly not force-broken to it—before they are hunting enthusiastically and pointing staunchly. Therefore, if your pup is one of the pointing breeds, it is best to shelve all thoughts of retrieving for a while. Don't be impatient; there'll be lots of time for retrieving later.

You may still be wondering about how and when you can safely indoctrinate a pointing breed pup to the sound of a gun going off. A pointer pup, or young dog, should be in full chase of a bird flushed in the field when the sound of gunfire is first heard. During your pup's early trips afield, if he begins enthusiastically chasing every bird he flushes, you can certainly give some thought to firing a cap pistol while he's chasing a bird some 75 feet away.

Discretion, rather than impatience, should rule your decision. If your pup has proved beyond doubt his boldness and precociousness, then, by all means, try popping a cap while he's really shagging a bird. If the noise elicits no perceptible reaction, you're ahead and can repeat the cap-popping at the next similar opportunity. But should your puppy show any nervousness—such as stopping cold and not continuing to chase, or coming right in to you, obviously unhappy about the noise—stroll on nonchalantly, but don't fire the cap gun again for the rest of that outing.

Gunshyness is a pitiable fault to observe in any kind of hunting dog. Not only does it make the dog utterly useless in the field, but it also brings a certain sense of failure to his owner, because it is a man-made fault. True, some puppies are susceptible to gunshyness, by virtue of a natural, inherited timidity, but susceptibility and contraction are two different things. All gun-shy dogs were made that way by some person; they did not enter the world afraid of gunfire.

The above is stated strongly so that it will serve as an admonition for you to proceed with some caution in introducing your pup to the noise of gunfire. Prevention of gunshyness is worth 50 pounds of cure, which, while not impossible, is very difficult and usually must be done by a professional trainer.

If your pup demonstrates timidity of loud noises, if he's jumpy or skittish, you must be prepared to wait until he's really fired up about chasing birds in the field—and has been doing so for some time—before you attempt to shoot even a cap gun in his vicinity. In the meantime, if you've noticed such jumpiness, have your family very gradually start rattling pots, pans, and dishes a bit more loudly around the pup as they go about their kitchen chores. Pay no attention to him if he rushes over to you for solace or slinks into his bed. Simply act as if you didn't even hear any noise and didn't notice the pup's reaction either. Such conditioning may take time, but it should pave the way for him to accept the sound of gunfire later on.

Assuming you've been able to get your pup afield several times a week for a couple of months, and have simultaneously gotten him well conditioned to his whole environment while also familiarizing him with the basic commands, by the time he's about five or six months of age he should be pretty well civilized.

CHAPTER 7

YOUR PUP'S YARD-TRAINING

Yard-training is just another expression meaning the formal instruction given a dog to teach him to understand and obey the commands most commonly used in the field and elsewhere. In short, it is instruction in basic obedience. Much of what is taught in yard-training can actually be accomplished indoors.

As in practically any aspect of bird dog training, there are diverse opinions about the timing and formality of yard-training a canine pupil. Some authorities, especially those of a field trial bent, advocate waiting until a dog has hunted a full season and reached close to peak enthusiasm for bird hunting before laying any serious obedience lessons on him. To do so prematurely, they contend, will generally rob a dog of his fullest desire to hunt and tend to make him develop in a more mechanical manner, one that lacks independence, fire, and drive, qualities admired and sought in both the field trial and high-class shooting dog.

Other experts believe that unless obedience is drummed into the pupil at the earliest possible opportunity total control will never be established and the dog will, just as often as not, do as he pleases. Somewhere in between these two philosophies there is a compromise, which is where the average bird dog owner can position himself and feel comfortable.

There exists a reasonable amount of latitude with respect to timing and formality. No one can say precisely what prescription will prove to be right for your pup. You will have to judge him yourself, depending largely on the rapport you've established with him and the intuitive knowledge you've gained of his personality.

As nearly as important will be the boldness and the degree of hunting desire your pup exhibits afield. If he seems too dependent on you, too loathe to range out as far as other pups of his type, breed, and age, then you'd be wiser to give him more time to catch up before beginning serious yard-training. Perhaps, too, in analyzing your pup, you should not forget to take a look at yourself. Make certain you've been doing your part in getting him to the field, in giving him the right kinds of opportunities, as often as possible. If you haven't, resolve to do so—and stick with your resolutions.

In general, yard-training can be undertaken with average pups between six and ten months old. Much of what is involved you will already have taught the pup informally. The big difference now, however, will be that your instructions will be more formalized, your demands more insistent, and your dog's compliance more disciplined. You should give profuse petting and praise as rewards for proper performance, but only words intoning disapproval for poor performance. There will be some pressure and some coercion, both of very mild persuasion.

Before trying to teach your dog something new, spend a minute or two reviewing a lesson he has down pat. This will bolster his confidence and gain him your praise and approval, better setting him up psychologically to learn a new command. Remember, also, to keep your sessions fairly brief. Two ten-minute lessons a day are about all the average adolescent pup can take without being pushed too hard.

During his early home life you will have familiarized him with such basics as his name and the commands, "No," "Here," "Sit," "Stay," "Kennel," and "All Right." The methods of teaching these commands, and several others, are as follows, and the only differences to be noted between their implementation for "familiarization" and "yard-training" are the degree of coercion and/or pressure involved.

NO!

A rudimentary command, "No" is an admonition with which your puppy will begin to become familiar about five minutes after he's arrived in your home. It is not a command taught in a formal manner. Rather, it usually involves physically stopping your puppy from committing an unwanted action, such as chomping on an article of clothing or some other household item. Whenever he's committing some transgression—and the number and variety are just short of being astronomical where a young pup is concerned—you should go to him, restrain him firmly, and while removing the article from his mouth, tell him "No" in a sharp tone of voice.

After reasonable repetition of the word has convinced you that its meaning is clear to your pup, emphasis can be added to the spoken command by rapping him on the snout with one or two fingers. Later, when he's reached five or six months of age, you can substitute the end of a leather leash or a flushing whip.

HERE!

Theoretically, teaching a pup to come to the call of a master he loves and trusts is one of the most easily accomplished lessons. In dealing

The command "Here" is best taught formally with a 25- or 50-foot check cord attached to your dog's collar. Kneeling down and getting closer to the dog's level encourages obedience. Photo by Robert Elman.

Above, left:
Teaching your dog to "Sit" on command is easy. With the dog on leash at your left side, place your left hand just forward of his hips, thumb on one side and fingers on the other, and squeeze gently as you apply downward pressure. Simultaneously, pull up on the leash, keeping it taut as you order your dog by name to "Sit." Photo by Robert Elman.

Above, right:
A variation of the position of the left hand spreads the fingers over a greater portion of the dog's back. In teaching him to sit, repeat the order several times and keep him sitting for about 30 seconds before releasing him with the "All Right" command. Photo by Robert Elman.

Opposite, top left:
Eventually, you should have your dog sitting not only on the verbal command, but also with a hand signal. The proper signal is given with your right arm fully extended, slightly above your head, with hand waggling in the manner of waving. At close range, for picture purposes, the hand is held only waist-high. Photo by Robert Elman.

Opposite, top center:
The dog is taught to "Stay" by first ordering him to sit. As he does, tell him by name "Stay." Move slowly in front of him, holding the leash barely taut with rearward pressure, and firmly repeat "Stay." As you move, extend your right hand, finger poised in a cautioning manner toward the pup.

Above, top right:
At first, a step or two away is all you'll be able to take before he tries to move, but you still have enough leverage to exert slight rearward pressure on the leash as you warn him, "Stay." Photo by Robert Elman.

Above, bottom left:
Soon you'll be able to make a complete circle around the dog at the outermost limits of the leash when you order him to "Stay." Photo by Robert Elman.

Above, bottom right:
Later, begin dropping the leash and increasing the distance between you and your dog. Photo by Robert Elman.

135

with the young puppy indoors, the standard procedure involves calling your pup by name, followed by the order, "Here," when you're about to feed or offer him some obvious reward—bribe might actually be a more accurate term.

Basically, there's no reason not to utilize this simple method. "Making him an offer he can't refuse" certainly has a lot to recommend it. By all means, use it both indoors and out in the initial stages of familiarization. Begun early enough, the conditioning aspects should prove useful for later training.

The problem outdoors will manifest itself soon enough when your dog—unrestrained and thoroughly interested in something highly intriguing—figuratively thumbs his nose at your "Here" command. While he's young, you can always slap your thigh to gain his attention, and again calling his name and the command, make an exaggerated show of running away from him. Many times such action is irresistible and the young puppy will come bounding after you. When he gets close enough to grab, reach out and stop him gently, repeating the command, "Here," while making a huge fuss over him.

This procedure doesn't always work with a dog five or six months of age or older, however, and if you can't enforce compliance to the recall order you will be sowing the seeds of serious problems. Therefore, the best way to teach the dog to always come when called is by use of a lightweight 25- or 50-foot check cord attached to his collar. With the cord trailing loosely, the dog will pay little attention to it. But if he doesn't respond immediately to your "Here," order, you can tactfully pressure him, pulling ever so gently as you repeat his name and the command until he's all the way in at your feet, where you can tell him what a good dog he is and make him feel rewarded for "obeying."

As your dog learns to respond quickly to your recall, you should begin injecting a whistle signal along with your vocal order. Generally, a long, trilling note is used as the signal to bring a dog in to you. Each time you tell him "Here," use your whistle. Eventually, he'll return to you on the whistle signal alone, which will save wear and tear on your voice later on in the field. (Incidentally, all the implements needed for the successful training of a bird dog are described and discussed in detail in Chapter 8.)

SIT!

The command, "Sit," is probably the easiest order for a man to teach and for his dog to learn. As a control command it is vital in handling a spaniel or retriever. Spaniel trainers seldom use the word "Sit," preferring the term "Hup," which, for some inexplicable reason, seems to evoke a quicker response—even in other breeds that are unfamiliar with the command. If you're a spaniel owner, "Hup" is the correct command to use; if you own a retriever, "Sit" is the proper one, although we still believe that "Hup" is more effective when using your dog as a flusher of upland birds.

When taught to pointing breeds, "Sit" is conventional for getting them to put their rumps on the ground. Many field trial buffs never teach their pointing dogs the command at all, believing that it interferes with the dog's early reaction to properly learning "Whoa," the most important of all field commands for pointing breeds. There is a chance, of course, that if taught to sit before learning to whoa, a somewhat edgy pointing dog might be more inclined to plop his fanny down when given a forceful "Whoa." Yet, because the "Sit" command is so simple for a dog to learn, it should be utilized to accustom a pointing breed puppy to learning something he can grasp very readily. It bolsters his self-confidence and is a good beginning for every formal training session.

Teaching your puppy to sit on command is best done by placing him on leash at your left side, assuming you're right-handed. If you're a port-sider, merely reverse the position. Place your left hand just forward of his hips, thumb on one side and fingers on the other, and squeeze gently as you simultaneously apply downward pressure. At the same time, pull up on the leash, keeping it taut as you order "Sit," preceded by his name. Keep your pup in the sitting position about thirty seconds, repeating the order and telling him "Good Boy" three or four times. Your praise, as always, should be intoned very happily.

Your pup should always be told "All Right" or "OK" when you want to release him from a previous command that requires your approval to resume whatever he may have been doing. Just be consistent and stay with whichever command you decide upon.

When you've kept your pup in the sitting position for about thirty seconds, release him and wait a minute before repeating the command "Sit." Proceed as above and continue the entire sequence perhaps five or six times more prior to ending the lesson. In subsequent sessions, you should find that he sits with just a tap of your hand on his back when you give him the command. Soon, the vocal order alone should suffice to make him obey.

Under no circumstances permit the young dog to ignore your command to sit—or, for that matter, any other command—as soon 137

. If he doesn't comply immediately, use the upward
ash and the downward push and squeeze of the hand to
assume the position ordered. As he demonstrates both a
.derstanding of your command and a willingness to obey,
keep him sitting for progressively longer periods before releasing
him. After each release, pile on the petting and compliments; after
all, pleasing you is the reward he seeks.

STAY

The meaning of the command "Stay" is clear. It tells your dog that
he must remain where he is, not changing position until so ordered.
Usually, it is utilized as a supplementary instruction to the order to
sit or lie down. Although some owners regard it as superfluous,
contending that the command "Sit" or "Down" implies staying in
those respective positions until released, actually the use of the order
"Stay" emphasizes and reinforces the previously given command.
It thus makes the trainer's job of teaching and the dog's job of
learning a little bit easier.

To begin the lesson, order your pup to sit. As he does, tell him, by
name, "Stay." Move slowly to his front, holding the leash barely
taut with slight rearward pressure, repeating firmly the order to stay.
As you move, extend your right hand with finger poised in a cautioning manner toward the pup. At first, you may only be able to take a
step or so away from your dog before he tries to move toward you. If

Above, left:
*Once you've gotten your dog from the sitting position to the down
position, keep him there with your left hand and repeat "Down"
along with lots of praise. Photo by Robert Elman.*
Above, right:
*To teach your dog to "Heel," you'll need a choke chain collar and a
leash at least 6 feet long. Step off smartly with the dog at your left
side, commanding him by name to "Heel." If he tries to bound
ahead, he'll put tension on the choke collar. Twirling the free end of
the leash in a vertical circle will also discourage his forging forward.
Photo by Robert Elman.*
Below:
*Teaching a pointing dog to "Whoa" really should be begun
informally indoors at his feed pan. If he doesn't understand or obey
the order outdoors, you'll have to resort to a long leash or check cord
and the method described in the text and illustrated here. Photo by
Robert Elman.*

he does attempt to come to you, you still have sufficient leverage to exert slight pressure toward his rear with the leash as you admonish him to "Stay."

Gradually, as the pup responds in a positive manner, increase the distance you back away from him, still holding the leash loosely and keeping your hand extended, while remaining alert to repeat the "Stay" order if he fidgets. Should he move, take him back to the exact spot from which he broke and give the command "Sit" and "Stay." Eventually, you should be able to make a complete circle around the dog at the outermost limits of the leash.

When the pup will stay riveted to the spot while you walk around him holding the leash, begin dropping the leash and increasing the distance between you and him. As before, if he breaks, simply back up in your sequence, resorting once again to replacing him in the original spot, commanding "Sit" and "Stay" and holding onto the leash as you circle him.

As your pup demonstrates good progress obeying your "Sit" and "Stay" orders, you can begin utilizing hand and whistle signals to a greater degree. For example, when you tell him to sit, fully extend your right arm, with palm up, slightly above your head and waggle your hand as if you're waving. Once your pup associates the motion with your verbal order, it won't take long for him to begin sitting at just the hand signal. The same is true of the "Stay" command coupled with your outstretched arm and cautioning finger.

If your pup is a flushing type, you'll have to teach him to "Hup" or "Sit" at a single sharp blast of the whistle. If he's a pointing breed, he should "Whoa" at that signal, something we'll delve into a bit farther along.

To teach your spaniel or retriever to sit at the proper whistle signal, you should backtrack to the procedure outlined earlier for instructing him to sit. In other words, put him on leash at your left side and go through the basic steps, the only difference being the introduction of the sharp single toot of the whistle just before you command "Sit." If you're able to work with him for ten minutes daily, or even four or five times a week, you should have him sitting at the whistle pretty reliably within seven or eight sessions. As with the earlier lessons, you can gradually increase the distance you work from your pup, extending or reducing it, according to his progress.

DOWN

Some owners don't bother with the "Down" command. What it means is for the dog to lie down, although some persons use it to order a dog who has jumped up on them to get all four feet back on the ground. Some trainers prefer the all-encompassing "No." However, the "Down" command is a practical one if you desire a perfectly behaved house dog, one that can be kept in a nonobnoxious attitude when necessary.

In the field it is a leftover from the days of muzzle-loaded fowling pieces, when a hunter had to keep his dog close at hand while laboriously reloading his gun before resuming the hunt. Then, the order was "Charge," appropriately describing what the hunter had to do to his firearm. Even today, a few old-timers can still be heard giving their dogs the order "Charge" when they stop to have a smoke or take a lunch break.

If you wish to teach your pup to lie down on command, put him on leash and order him to sit. When he's in the proper position, at your left side, place your left hand just in back of his shoulder blades, thumb on the right and fingers on the left. Then, in much the same way you taught him to sit, exert gentle pressure, by simultaneously squeezing and pushing downward on his shoulders as you say his name and command, "Down." Should he resist too strenuously, briskly slide your right forearm behind his front legs and, with quick dexterity, force them straight out from under him.

Once he's down, keep him there with your left hand while you praise him and pet him soothingly with your right. When he seems to accept this comfortable position, release him with an "All Right," and continue your walk. Try him again a minute or so later, with a crisp "Down" order. Assuming you're not lucky, merely repeat the original sequence, ordering him to sit, and resuming the procedure outlined above until he complies or until the lesson is ended.

Ultimately, when he understands and obeys the "Down" command, you can introduce a hand signal, using it each time you order him down. The signal we prefer consists of extending the first finger of the right hand and pointing toward the ground, pumping the forearm two or three times in that direction.

KENNEL

Another of the most rudimentary commands, "Kennel" is doubtless the most universally used order telling a dog to "get in" to something. Excluding mischief, the command directs your dog to enter into a wide variety of things—cars, houses, boats, carrying crates, dog beds, dog houses, kennel runs, etc. It is obviously a very necessary directive for home and field.

141

Like "No," the order to "Kennel" is not taught in a formal manner; rather, it is habituated gradually. Each time you put your pup into his crate or bed, the car, or kennel run, simply command "Kennel." He'll soon learn that the word means "get in," although he won't necessarily obey until you demonstrate to him that he has no choice in the matter. This you'll do, at first, by physically putting him into the object in question. When there's not the slightest doubt that he knows what you want, but decides willfully to ignore your order, a rap on the rump with flushing whip or leather leash should suffice to make him hop to.

HEEL

If you've ever watched someone trying to walk an exuberant but undisciplined Great Dane down a city street, you may have wondered just who was walking whom. Even a smaller dog tugging for all he's worth at the end of a leash can cause his owner discomfort or, worse yet, in slippery going, a bad fall.

On the other hand, a dog walking mannerly at heel is a pleasure to see or own, and seldom, if ever, is responsible for mishap to himself or his owner. Such a dog is under better control and more receptive to whatever commands may be issued.

Despite the belief by some trainers that teaching a dog to heel should not be attempted until he reaches the age of six to ten months, we prefer familiarizing a pup with the command and its meaning at about three-and-a-half months. Naturally, like most of the other "familiarization" training given a pup that young, there should never be any punishment or rough handling involved. Such early training will help to condition the puppy to the more disciplined instruction given him later in the yard.

In the informal stages, you should encourage the young pup to walk on leash on either your left or right side, depending upon whether you're a rightie or a leftie. Conventionally, the right-hander works his dog at his left side. Everytime you snap the leash on your pup to take him outdoors, or out of his kennel, line him up about even with your left knee, slap your leg and, saying his name, command, "Heel," as you begin walking.

While he's young, you won't have too much difficulty in keeping apace with him. Whenever he surges ahead, tug firmly on the leash as you tell him, "Heel." Do the same thing if he lags behind or gets too far offside, but be careful not to sour your pup on heeling at such a tender age.

Ideally, try to get him to walk at heel only for a distance of about 30 to 40 feet—say from your doorway to the spot where he usually relieves himself—before releasing him with an "All Right." Then, after he's taken care of his needs and you're ready to walk back to the house, repeat the procedure once more.

In the more serious yard-training lessons, when he is between six and ten months old, teaching him to "Heel" will take a bit more coercion to convince him he must obey the order, without hesitation, everytime you give it. To accomplish this, you'll need a chain choke collar and a leash at least 6 feet long. The choke collar, sometimes called a slip-chain collar, tightens around the dog's neck as he pulls; the more he pulls, the more the collar tightens.

Follow the earlier procedure, lining your pup up with your left knee, slapping your thigh, and saying his name as you command, "Heel." Step off smartly and begin twirling the free end of the leash in a vertical circle. If your dog tries to bound ahead, not only will he put tension on his collar but also get rapped in the snoot by the continuously swinging leash. Whenever he forges forward, lags behind, or moves too far to the side, simply jerk the leash sharply with your left hand and tell him, "Heel."

It will take a while for him to learn to heel happily, but once he realizes that there is no discomfort from the choke collar or the swinging leash when he heels properly, he should conform willingly. When he does, you can soon begin working him without the leash snapped to his collar. As long as he continues to heel correctly, you can consider this lesson successfully learned. Should he break and leave your side, though, you will have no recourse but to return to use of the leash and choke collar until he's readily complying once again.

WHOA

If your pup is one of the pointing breeds, no other command is more important than "Whoa" in making him a useful bird dog. What "Hup" or "Sit" is to the flushing breeds, "Whoa" is to the pointing dogs. The order should halt a dog in his tracks and keep him frozen in position until he's released. It is the most vital control factor available to the pointing dog owner.

Like many of the foregoing commands taught in yard-training, "Whoa" can and should be introduced into the pointing breed puppy's familiarization training as early as possible, usually around his fourteenth to sixteenth week. Acquainting him with the meaning of the command is most easily accomplished at feeding time, when his incentive of a food reward makes him particularly eager to please.

The procedure is simple. Restrain the puppy with one hand as you set his pan of chow on the floor, a couple of feet away, with the other. Naturally, he'll make a strong attempt to get to his food. Tell him, by name, softly, soothingly, "Whoa," while you hold one hand on his chest, between his forelegs, and keep his rear elevated by grasping the root of his tail with the other. This will not hurt the pup if you get a handle on his tail right where it joins his stern.

Gradually, as he calms down, continue holding one hand on his chest and begin stroking his back gently with the other, all the while quietly saying "Whoa," and praising him if he stands pat. Should he try to sit down, raise him easily into a standing position, repeating his name and the command. When you have him whoaing for about twenty or thirty seconds, tap him lightly on the back of the head and tell him, "All Right," which will release him to go and eat his food.

Since he'll be eating three meals a day at three-and-a-half or four months of age, you'll have ample opportunities to familiarize your pup with the command. Never punish or hassle him during these informal sessions; rather, attempt to show him in as gentle a fashion as possible what "Whoa" means, and that it actually portends something enjoyable. Later on, in the field, it will normally precede your flushing a bird he's pointed staunchly.

When you get to the serious and formalized teaching of "Whoa" in the yard, you'll need a long leash or check cord. Since he already should have been well indoctrinated in the meaning of the order, try it out on him after you've run through one or two of the lessons he's previously learned. Tell him to Whoa. Without the stimulus of his feed pan, he might not obey. Jerk the leash or check cord sharply and repeat the directive. If he does whoa then, go to him and, in honeyed tones, let him know what a great dog he is, while reassuringly stroking him. Keep him standing immobile as you praise and pet him and repeatedly command "Whoa," softly. After half-a-minute, release him with an "All Right" and a tap on the head.

As in all other training lessons, repetition and consistency are the keys to success. When your dog demonstrates his understanding of and desire to obey the "Whoa" command, you can start extending the distance at which the order is given, ultimately dropping the leash or check cord and keeping him glued in position while you walk a complete circle around him.

Should your dog experience difficulty in comprehending the "Whoa" command outdoors, there is a simple expedient you can use

Let your dog's yard-training proceed at a pace best suited to your teaching ability and your dog's learning capacity. Most important, remember to give lavish praise for a job well done and always end every lesson on a happy note. Photo by Robert Elman.

that generally succeeds. A long leash will do, but a check cord is really better for the job. With your dog on the check cord, walk him to a tree or fence post and, as he passes the obstacle, make sure you stay on the opposite side of it and command, "Whoa." Since you'll be holding the cord, if your dog tries to move toward you, he'll encounter the rearward resistance exerted on the cord by the obstacle behind him.

Gradually, you can back away from him, keeping slight tension on the cord as you slide it through your hand. (A note of caution: always wear gloves when working a dog on a check cord to avoid any chance of rope burn.) Keep him in the whoa position for at least thirty seconds, cautioning him both by voice and with arm extended, palm upraised, before going to him to release him. It's important that you walk to your dog to release him from the "Whoa" command with a tap on the head and an "All Right," rather than letting him come to you.

Anytime your dog moves from the original spot at which you ordered him to whoa, you will have to go to him and replace him in that exact spot. Once he begins whoaing properly, you can introduce the whistle signal to whoa—a single, short, sharp blast—along with the spoken order. Eventually, of course, he will learn to obey either one as soon as he hears it.

Yard-training your bird dog, whether he be pointer, spaniel, or retriever, is something to which you must be prepared to devote a reasonable amount of time. What you are attempting to teach your dog are commands he must know, understand, and obey for the remainder of his life, either at home or afield, in order to be a good canine citizen, as well as a serviceable bird dog.

Take the time and make the effort to instruct him with proper patience and perseverance. What he has to learn cannot be soaked up quickly, like water in a sponge. So don't try to push him too fast. Neither you nor he is on an inflexible schedule, striving to meet any deadline on progress. Let progress proceed at a practical pace, one that best seems to suit your teaching ability and your dog's learning capacity.

CHAPTER 8

FIELD
TRAINING
EQUIPMENT

Many of the implements needed to train a bird dog successfully have undergone little change in a century or more, indicating the practicability of the essential accessories and the fact that design improvements of traditional equipment come about solely through sheer necessity. On the other hand, there is a growing list of new training tools, largely the result of modern technology, designed to simplify and accelerate the trainer's job. Some of these devices can only be described as innovative marvels, tools that can accomplish wonders when correctly used.

Here, we intend to look at both varieties. You will not need every piece of equipment discussed, but you should know that such items exist and what purposes they serve. Decide for yourself which implements—beyond the basic ones—may prove of specific value to you, after you've gained more experience afield in training your dog.

First, let's concentrate on the traditional, essential items.

THE COLLAR

The various types of collars available, designed for a variety of functions, can best be categorized as "everyday" and "training" collars. The former should always be worn by your dog when he's outside the house. Some people prefer that their dogs wear collars at all times. Naturally, such collars should have attached to them a metal identification plate inscribed with your name, address, and telephone number, in the event your dog ever strays or gets lost.

The collar provides you with a means of controlling your dog, on or off leash. In the everyday variety, collars are available in round or flat leather, flat nylon, and chain link types. The round ones customarily are favored for longhaired bird dogs, whereas the flat types are generally chosen for short-coated breeds. The chain link kind, which comes in full or partial choke collar, can be used on any bird dog, and doubles as a training collar. It is not, however, a safe collar for hunting or field-training purposes, because of its predilection for getting hung up on brush and barbed-wire fences.

The training collar can be of three different types: the regular, full or partial choke chain collar; the full chain choker with double row blunted metal prongs around the inside; and the wide leather force-training or J.A.S.A. spike collar with a zigzag row of semiblunted prongs circling the inside.

The choke chain collar, either full or partial type, is most useful for yard-training puppies and adult dogs of mild or average temperament. It is designed, in nooselike fashion, to tighten around the dog's neck if tension is applied by hand or with a leash, and to loosen as soon as tension is slackened.

The full chain choker with double row blunted metal prongs is usually reserved for yard-training adult dogs of somewhat fractious nature. Its principle is the same as that of the choke collar, but, of course, has the added inducement of metal prongs that pinch the dog's neck harmlessly but effectively. This collar is also used to force train dogs to retrieve and to teach pointing dogs to be staunch on point and steady to wing and shot.

The force-training or J.A.S.A. spike collar is similar in design and purpose to the full chain choker. Constructed of wide, heavy leather, with a row of semiblunted metal prongs set in zigzag pattern on the inside, this nooselike collar is used by professional trainers in "breaking" recalcitrant adult dogs. Like the chain choker, it can also be employed in force training dogs to retrieve. It is seldom necessary for the average amateur trainer to resort to using a spike collar unless he has an unusually hardheaded and thick-skinned dog.

THE LEASH

Several varieties of leashes are available, but the one thing they all share in common is the ability they give the trainer to restrain and control his dog. The main differences in leashes are length and type of material, some being as short as 10 inches or as long as 10 feet, and constructed of tough plastic, with a wire core; nylon; chain; leather—or a combination of the latter two materials.

The very short leashes—10 to 20 inches—are specialized-use items strictly for leading adult dogs for short distances. The medium-length leashes—3 to 5 feet—serve nicely as everyday types for walking your dog. Leashes from 5 to 10 feet long are generally the sort used for training purposes.

In our opinion, the best kind of training leash is made of quality leather, about ¾ inch width, and approximately 8 feet long. This is the type of leash, or lead, as it is often called, that is most valuable when you begin yard-training your six- to ten-month-old pup.

Probably the best general-purpose leash, for field, home, and training, is a combination of leather in the upper two-thirds and chain in the lower third, the total length measuring about 6 feet. Such construction allows for reasonable lightness, while preventing the weakening effects of chewing on the portion closest to the dog.

Excluded from consideration here, of course, are the very small and lightweight collars and leashes you should use on a six- to ten-week old puppy—the kind you first bring home.

THE WHISTLE

Since whistle signals play a vital part in controlling a bird dog in the field, a good whistle is a must. Numerous types of whistles are available, most of them suitable for training and field use. Various materials, such as bone, stag horn, metal, plastic, and Bakelite, are used in their manufacture. Our personal preference is plastic or Bakelite since, unlike metal, these materials won't stick to your lips in very cold weather.

Forget the so-called silent whistles; you can't hear them and, consequently, won't be able to develop the signal variations required to control and direct your dog in the field. Among the most popular whistles are the police-type, which contain a tiny round ball of cork or plastic that permits the user to produce a wide variety of signal nuances. The most satisfactory and best-known whistles are the Acme Thunderer and Roy Gonia brands. An excellent choice for signaling wide-ranging pointing dogs, particularly under windy conditions, is the long-distance whistle made by the National Scent Company of Garden Grove, California. A short lanyard is customarily used to hang one or more whistles around your neck.

THE CHECK CORD

Without doubt, the check cord is one of the most useful items in the bird dog trainer's kit. Its purpose is clearly indicated in its name—to check, or restrain, a dog in the yard or afield. A check cord can be made of any number of different materials; clothesline, hemp, nylon, and braided poly are some examples. Lengths can vary widely, especially among the home-made variety, but the most popular ones are 25, 50, 75, and 100 feet long.

For yard-training, or working a dog in heavy cover, a 25-footer should normally suffice. For most field-training, a 50-foot cord proves to be best. The extra-long 75- and 100-foot check cords can be used most effectively in big fields of light cover, where the pointing dog is inclined to range fairly wide. The extra-long cords are also useful in teaching the flushing dog to quarter his ground within specific distances.

THE BLANK CARTRIDGE GUN

To accustom your dog to the sound of gunfire in the field, the blank cartridge gun is a must. It is used when your dog makes contact with and is enthusiastically chasing either game birds or song birds. The most commonly preferred blank guns are .22 caliber revolver-type starter guns holding six or eight blanks in a swing-out cylinder. Eventually, the blank gun should take the place of the cap gun while your pup is retrieving thrown dummies.

Above:
The implements most often used to train a bird dog include (from left to right, starting at the bottom): 8-foot leather leash; .22 caliber blank-cartridge revolver; whistle and lanyard; flushing whip; regular leather collar encircling dog bell; 50-foot check cord with leather handle loop; kapok-filled canvas retrieving dummy; J.A.S.A. leather force-training collar with spikes, and a quail harness with blunted prongs.
Below, left:
The J.A.S.A. leather force-training collar is used by professional trainers in "breaking" recalcitrant adult dogs. Unless you have an unusually hardheaded, thick-skinned dog, forget this collar.
Below, right:
A good whistle is vital to the bird-dog trainer. This is a long-distance whistle, made by the National Scent Company, Garden Grove, Calif., attached to a short lanyard.

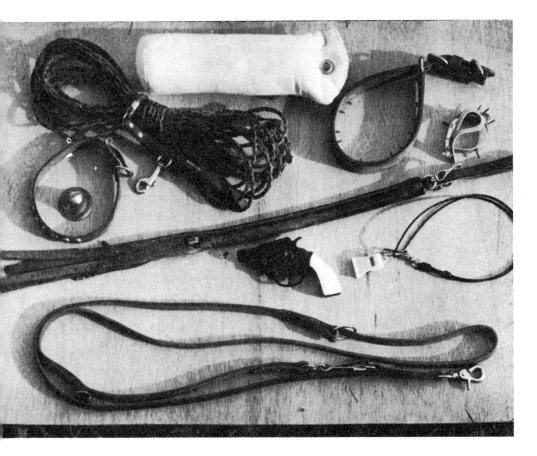

THE RETRIEVING DUMMY

An important implement in teaching your bird dog to fetch is the retrieving dummy. Commercially available in various types and sizes, dummies look like smaller versions of the boat fenders seamen use to protect their crafts' gunwales. The most favored type is kapok-filled heavy canvas with a grommet at the top, to which a length of rope can be rigged for easier tossing.

Such canvas dummies float well in water, are rugged enough to use on land, and retain quite well commercial training scents applied to them. Besides being thrown for dogs to fetch, training dummies are also useful as "artificial birds." Fitted with two or more pairs of game bird wings (wrapped with heavy monofilament or taped flat against it), a dummy can be stashed in heavy grass and your dog encouraged to hunt for a dead bird.

THE FLUSHING WHIP

The standard flushing whip, made of leather casing over a spring or strip of flat metal to give it body with flexibility, can be a handy item for any bird dog trainer. The lower third, which is about 10 inches long and contains no spring or metal innards, consists of one or more leather straps. The opposite end generally has a wrist loop and a bolt snap for convenient carrying on the belt.

Used to flail the ground cover to flush tight-sitting birds, the flushing whip also can serve as a short, convenient field leash for leading dogs short distances at heel. In addition, the flushing whip makes an ideal disciplinary tool for giving a willfully disobedient dog a good sting on the rump.

Above:
A must to condition your bird dog to the sound of gunfire is an ordinary .22 caliber blank cartridge revolver.
Center:
The kapok-filled canvas retrieving dummy is a necessary tool to keep your bird dog in practice fetching. Adding a few drops of commercially manufactured liquid scent of the bird you're most interested in hunting helps condition your dog to that odor.
Below:
A dog bell attached to his collar is handy to help you keep tabs on your dog's whereabouts in dense cover.

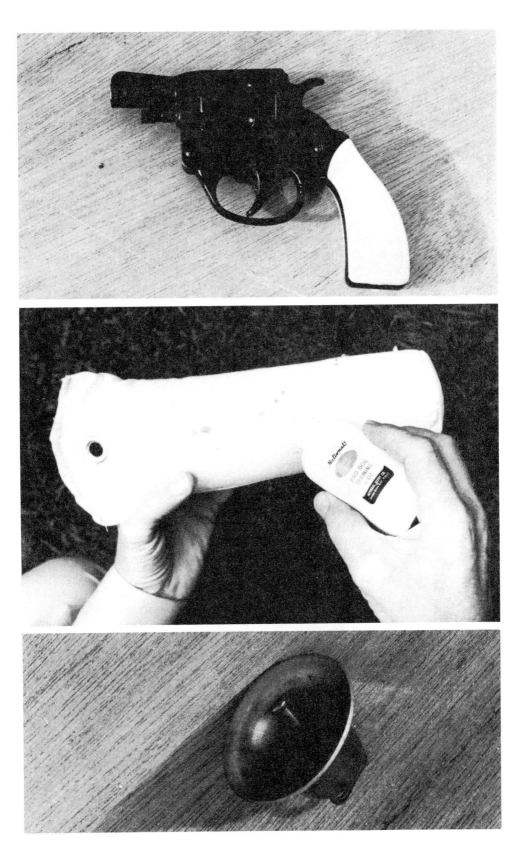

TRAINING SCENTS

Training scents, manufactured commercially in concentrated liquid form that duplicates the body effluvia of most of the principal game birds, are useful in several ways, especially in introducing young pups to the smell of the bird or birds you're most interested in hunting. The scent of your choice can be applied to a canvas training dummy with which you're teaching your dog to retrieve, familiarizing him with that scent every time he fetches the dummy. Wrapped with game bird wings, as described earlier, and daubbed with several drops of scent, a dummy can be secreted in dense grass and your puppy sent to find the "bird."

Other scent compounds—of animals such as deer or rabbit that your bird dog should ignore—are called "breaking scents." Customarily, they are doused on small, commercially available scent pads that snap onto a dog's collar, where, saturated daily and left for several days, the smell eventually becomes abhorrent to the dog.

THE DOG BELL

Although not a training implement, the dog bell is a valuable accessory, enabling a trainer or hunter to keep tabs on his dog's whereabouts when he's working in dense cover. If your dog is one of the pointing breeds, and he's belled, you will know he's on point when the bell quits tinkling. On the flushing breeds, a bell also serves as a good indicator of what the dog is doing; instead of stopping when a bird is located, the bell will jingle faster as the flushing dog excitedly begins making game.

THE ELECTRONIC SHOCK COLLAR

The purpose of the remote-controlled electronic shock collar is to deliver an uninjurious yet highly astonishing electric shock to a dog at the moment he's committing a misdeed. The distance at which the shock can be delivered is considerable, and it can be accomplished at the mere pushing of a button—an awesome amount of power in the hands of the trainer.

The unit consists of a lightweight, battery-operated transmitting device, held by the trainer, and a small receiver, equipped with a shocking coil, fitted to a leather collar worn by the dog. When the transmitter button is pushed, a radio signal is directed to the receiver in the collar, where a tiny switch triggers the coil and creates an

Left:
The remote-controlled electronic shock collar represents an awesome amount of power in the hands of any dog trainer. The collar unit on the left is worn by the dog while the trainer carries the transmitter.

Right:
When the trainer pushes a button on the transmitter, a radio signal is directed to a receiver in the dog's collar unit, delivering an immediate electric shock for as long as the button is depressed. The misuse of this device can cause untold problems.

155

immediate electric shock. The jolt, although harmless, is sufficiently startling to dissuade the dog from continuing his transgression.

Such a device has illimitable uses, such as deterring a dog from chasing deer, rabbits, or other unwanted game; discouraging a trained pointing dog from willfully breaking wing and shot to chase birds like a puppy; keeping a pointing or flushing dog from ranging too far; and correcting a dog that deliberately ignores the recall order, to cite just a few. The units also are valuable to curb the serious problem of car-chasing and the annoyance of chronic barking by a kennel dog.

Obviously, the electronic shock collar is valuable because it gives the trainer the ability to issue corrective punishment at a distance and at the precise moment the dog is committing his transgression. However, despite its multiplicity of uses, the shock collar is not a panacea, to be used imprudently in every problem situation. For many competent bird dog trainers, the shock collar is a device to be employed only as a last resort on dogs so recalcitrant that no other recourse remains. Certainly, in the hands of an amateur, it can be grossly misused. An electronic shock collar should only be used after considerable forethought; it is not a toy.

THE RELEASE TRAP

A varied assortment of release traps can be purchased today, ranging from the most simplistic in design and operation to the most futuristic and sophisticated. Their purpose, however, is the same: to contain a live pigeon or game bird safely and release it to fly, when the trainer so wishes.

Some of these traps are made of wire, some of wood, some of metal. All of them feature a release mechanism that must be activated by the trainer. The most satisfactory type is the kind that pops open and, simultaneously, ejects its bird 5 or 6 feet into the air, giving it a flying head start and preventing a dog that's too close from catching it.

The most sophisticated and expensive release trap marketed at present is the Tri-Tronics Electronic Game Bird Releaser, which enables the dog handler to catapult a bird into the air, from as far away as 500 feet, at the press of a button on a hand-held transmitter. The operating principle is the same as that of the previously described electronic shock collar.

With this remote-controlled type of unit, or one having a long pull cord, both pointing and flushing breeds can be worked on birds effectively. The advantage of a release trap is that it permits total control over the location and time of release of the bird. If your dog is worked on a check cord, then, obviously, you also will have total control of him as well. The combination of the release trap and the check cord on your dog gives you about as much control in a live game bird training situation as is ever possible to attain. And the use of a release trap offers the advantage of being able to work on live game in a relatively small area.

There are also some disadvantages to the release trap. Most of the various models constructed of anything except wire mesh simply don't permit as much bird scent to escape as is desirable. Add to this the fact that the trap must be camouflaged with grass or other natural cover and the body scent may be further reduced. Of course, this situation can be overcome to some extent by tapping the live bird gently against the surrounding ground and cover before you place the bird in the trap.

THE ELECTRONIC BEEPER COLLAR

Though the beeper collar is similar in purpose to the plain old-fashioned dog bell, the electronic-age device deserves to be considered as much more than simply a high-technology bell appealing only to the gadget-minded dog owner. Actually, the beeper is a very skillfully engineered multi-function audio device that outperforms the ordinary dog bell six ways to Sunday.

Among the best of numerous beepers on the market is the Sonic PRO/XR. A roughly four-inch-long cylinder of thick-wall PVC tube construction affixed to an inch-wide orange Duralon collar, the unit is powered by a 9-volt Duracell battery.

Placed on the dog and switched on, the unit is ready to go to work, broadcasting its sequential two-note *Run & Point* signal. As long as the dog keeps moving, the PRO continues to sound at an adjustable rate, letting the gunner track his dog's movements no matter what the cover. When the dog stops, so does the sound, for a selectable 6- or 12-second delay. If he begins moving again, the run signal starts once more. But if he remains motionless, on point, a different tone signals approximately at 3-second intervals.

Selectable switches in the PRO enable numerous adjustments to customize the unit for dog and owner. And it's doubtful that the beeper is any more apt to spook birds than is an ordinary dog bell.

How loud is the PRO/XR beeper? Under most typical upland hunting conditions, an owner blessed with normal, average hearing should find

157

Operated by a 9-volt Duracell battery, the Sonic PRO/XR electronic beeper collar is rugged, lightweight, and has a number of state-of-the-art features.

the device audible for 200 yards or more. Naturally, factors such as wind, air temperature, and humidity can raise hob with any sound, but whenever a regular dog bell can be heard, even faintly, the PRO and, in fact, most beepers, will be clearly audible.

Waterproof and very ruggedly built, the PRO, with its many selectable and adjustable features, is clearly an invaluable state-of-the-art accessory for the upland gunner. Manufactured by ATS Electronic Products, 38-52 20th Avenue, Blanchard, MI 49310, the Sonic PRO/XR is available exclusively from the manufacturer.

Unlike an ordinary dog bell, the electronic beeper helps to locate a dog on point by emitting beeps at a different rate from the run signal. Under average conditions, most beepers can be heard at longer ranges than bells.

Lake, Minnesota 55025, the Tracker is only available directly from the manufacturer.

THE DUMMY LAUNCHER

Although it is seldom necessary for a pointing or flushing dog retrieving in the uplands to do any fetching at distances greater than 45 yards—and that's a long shot—there is a device available that launches dummies up to nearly twice that far. The "Retriev-R-Trainer" is a gadget that utilizes a .22 caliber blank cartridge charge to hurl a soft plastic training dummy as far as 250 feet away.

A metal rod in the bottom of the unit's handle serves as the trigger, making it a two-handed operation. Both the angle at which the device is held and the type of propelling charge (regular or heavy duty) determine how far the dummy is flung. Of course, it saves wear and tear on the pitching arm and seasons a dog to the noise of gunfire while giving him practice in marking distant falls.

THE BIRD HARNESS

In situations where wild game birds are scarce and your pup simply hasn't had sufficient opportunity to make live game contacts, a bird harness can be a real lifesaver. This device is a rig that can be fitted around a live bird, allowing it complete freedom of movement within the limitations of a length of cord. Coming in several sizes to fit pigeons, bobwhite quail, and even ring-necked pheasants, the bird harness is adjustable and has blunt studs judiciously positioned around the outside to prevent a dog from chomping down on the bird and injuring it.

In harness, a quail or pigeon can be attached, via a dee ring, to a length of strong monofilament secured to one end of a 10- or 12-foot bamboo pole and worked enticingly in front of a pup on a check cord. This enables the trainer to excite a pointing breed pup into a

The bird harness, fitted with blunted metal prongs, can be fitted around a live quail or pigeon. Although it is an artificial device, it can spell the difference between some bird work or none.

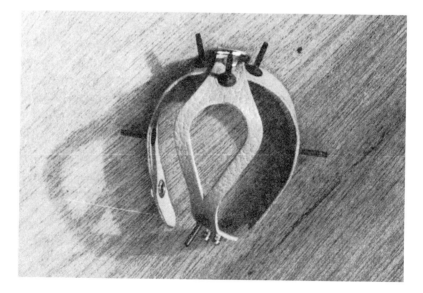

sight point, while at the same time letting him wind the bird so that he'll associate the act of pointing with the scent of a live bird. Similarly, the harnessed bird can be used to fire up a flushing breed pup, also worked on a check cord and encouraged to bore in hard and "flush" it—the act simulated, of course, when the trainer or an assistant pulls the bird into the air with the pole.

As was stated at the beginning of this chapter, you won't need all of the equipment we've discussed in order to train your bird dog successfully. Make sure, however, that you obtain the essential items. And, remember, bargain prices seldom turn out to be real bargains; don't stint on the training implements you'll have to depend upon to get the job done properly.

CHAPTER 9

INTRODUCTION TO HUNTING

By the time public hunting seasons open for game birds in most parts of North America—roughly in mid-October—the pup you brought home in late spring or early summer will probably be somewhere between five and eight months old. During those ensuing months, you will have pretty well ''civilized'' and established good rapport with him; given him sufficient time in the field; accustomed him to some type of gunfire; and probably begun some of his formal yard-training lessons.

Now that bird seasons are opening, you're anxious to get out there and ''pop a few caps.'' Can you, should you, take your puppy along? If so, what should you expect of him? Will actual hunting help or impair his progress? Will it interrupt or interfere with his continued training?

The answers to these questions must necessarily be conditional. At this juncture, your situation calls for a judgmental decision: should you do a lot of bird shooting and little training, or more training and less shooting?

If you choose the former, you may get lucky and wind up with a dog that, with lots of experience on birds, will virtually train himself. Or, more likely, by neglecting your pup over a whole season for the sake of shooting at every bird that flies, he may develop some very bad habits that may prove difficult to correct later.

Obviously, then, it would make better sense for you to look upon the open season as a continuation of his progress and not worry too much about having to sacrifice a good deal of your bird shooting during his first season in the field. In other words, take him hunting; the more opportunities he has to get afield and make contacts with birds, the better off he'll be. By hunting, we mean real hunting; take along your shotgun—nothing larger than 20 gauge though—and some light field loads, and be prepared to do some limited shooting under precisely the right conditions.

Whether your pup is a pointing or flushing type is immaterial; during his initial hunting season you should be striving mainly to awaken and stimulate to a maximum degree all his latent natural instincts for the chase. Getting him into birds, letting him chase and, eventually, mouth a few that you've shot for him should greatly excite his deep-rooted hunting desire. You'll also be instilling in him the confidence and independence the worthwhile bird dog always displays. This is not just a question of stylishness, but a real necessity if you want to develop an aggressive bird-finder, the only kind that produces consistently.

When we said you should plan to do more training and less shooting, by "training" we didn't mean issuing a continual barrage of commands and whistle signals, combined with constant correction and nagging. A better word, in this context, would be "supervision"—similar to the subliminal conditioning you practiced during your pup's preliminary field outings.

On his first few hunting trips, discipline should be kept to a bare minimum. If you can avoid situations that would demand your disciplining the pup, such as his willful disobedience of a command, do so. Whenever possible, try to anticipate what your pup is going to do a minute or two before the action occurs. Often, it will be something

Above:
Take your young dog along when the public hunting season opens. Carry a 20-gauge shotgun and light loads and shoot only under the right circumstances.
Below, left:
Keep discipline to a minimum on his first few hunting trips. Use your whistle sparingly and make it mean something. Photo by Robert Elman.
Below, right:
By getting your young dog into birds you'll further stimulate his hunting desire and enthusiasm for finding feathered game.

you can prevent by changing your direction and giving him the two-toot whistle and arm signal you taught him earlier.

One potential pitfall you must watch out for is imprudent shooting over your young dog. Make certain, just as you did during his preliminary field trips, that your pup is in full chase of a bird, and at least 20 to 25 yards away, before you fire your shotgun. Unless your pup is a spaniel or retriever who has already had a few pigeons shot for him to fetch, it's probable that this will be the first time he'll be hearing a shotgun go off. In the concentrated exhilaration of the moment—bird scent still hot in his nostrils and even hotter pursuit of the quarry underway—your dog probably won't even take notice of the noise.

Although it will be a deliberately longer than average shot, in order to make sure the pup isn't too close, pray that you kill the bird cleanly, so your pup will be right on it almost before it hits the ground. Let him mouth it a little and then urge him happily to bring the bird to you, telling him, by name, "Good boy, fetch here." With any luck, he'll trot in proudly with the bird. Get your hand on his collar, to keep him there with you, while you pet and praise him profusely, continuing to let him hold the bird.

Don't be in a hurry to take it from him; permit him to savor his moment of triumph. When you do take the bird, command "Give," and, if necessary, gently squeeze his lower lips against his teeth to make him relinquish it. After removing any loose feathers from your dog's mouth, toss the bird a few feet away and have him fetch it for you once more. Pour on the demonstrative joy again, then pocket the bird and double toot your whistle to start your dog hunting anew.

In this near-perfect sequence, you'll be accomplishing a number of important things. You'll have introduced your pup to the sound of a shotgun, killed a game bird—the act of which he'll associate with the gunfire—let him get his mouth on the bird and retrieve it for you.

But suppose you weren't that lucky; you missed the bird. If your dog evidenced signs that the single shotgun blast disturbed him,

---

Above:
Make certain your dog is in full chase and that his bird is well out before your shoot. Initially, limit yourself to one shot per bird to avoid any chance of creating gunshyness in your dog. Photo by Leonard Lee Rue III.
Below:
Killing cleanly the first bird your pup points, if he's a pointing breed, is vital. If he also retrieves it, be sure to heap on the praise.

although not seriously, what you should do is feign complete indifference to his edginess and, double-tooting him on with the whistle, continue hunting. Refrain from shooting at the next bird or two he finds and bumps so that his enthusiasm will return to full eagerness. When your next chance occurs, wait the bird out just a bit longer, but when you shoot, kill it. Then let him fetch it as already described.

On that same outing, if you are able to kill even one more bird for your pup and have him mouth and bring it in to you, consider yourself extremely fortunate. Even if your dog makes contact with a couple more birds that you don't have a shot at, the entire episode will have added immeasurably to his self-confidence as well as his zealousness for bird hunting. Each subsequent hunting trip will provide additional opportunities to intensify his hunting desire and increase his experience. But so, too, will each trip offer potentials for developing problems if you relax your vigilance.

Unless you have a hunting buddy who is very knowledgeable about bird dogs or very understanding after you brief him, you'll run far fewer risks by hunting your pup alone for the first season. One reason for this is to avoid too much shooting at one time over your pup. (The time-honored expression "shooting over" a dog means shooting in the company of, not literally "over" a dog's head— something that should never be done.) Remember, he's still only a youngster and not yet immune to becoming gunshy. A pup that shows no signs of having heard a single shot, or perhaps even two, may evidence distinct nervousness at the sound of three of four quick blasts. You should limit your shooting to one shot per bird until your pup has been hunting enough to disregard the sound of gunfire.

If you get your pup out as often as possible throughout the public

---

Above, left:
If you can kill more than one bird on your first hunt together and let your pup mouth or retrieve it, you'll be making great progress.
Above, right:
Eventually, if your dog is a pointing breed, only shoot at those birds on which he establishes point, even momentarily.
Below:
In the case of a flushing dog, refrain from shooting at any birds he puts up beyond gun range. This springer obviously did a fine job of finding, flushing, and retrieving a fat chukar partridge. Photo by John Madson.

open hunting season for birds, he will be learning a lot: where to search for birds; how to use his nose; how to take advantage of the breeze; how to follow body and foot scent; and, to some extent, how to approach and handle birds. This invaluable knowledge is not something you can teach him; only by hunting and finding birds can he develop the inherited instincts he was born with. Once he demonstrates that he's an eager beaver where birds are concerned, that he'd rather hunt than eat—which in large measure will depend on his age, type, breed, and individuality—you can begin taking a more formal attitude toward the way he hunts and start channeling his efforts into more functional service to the gun.

If your pup is a pointing breed, he should certainly have begun establishing flash points—momentary pauses of immobility—when he first locates a bird before breaking and causing the bird to take wing. Once he exhibits the insatiable urge to search for and find birds, you should refrain from shooting at any birds he bumps deliberately or accidentally, firing only at those he points, even for only twenty or thirty seconds. If you ignore those he does not take the time to point, he will soon get the message that the gunfire that comes about when he points means he'll get his mouth on a bird. Without the point, there will be no gunfire and, consequently, no bird to mouth.

Basically, the same psychology applies in the case of the spaniel or retrieving breed used as a flushing dog. Unless the dog gets his birds airborne within gun range, you should not senselessly continue popping caps. If you have been successful in getting your flushing dog to "Hup" or "Sit" on voice command or whistle signal, the chances are excellent that you'll be able to keep him hunting inside the 35- to 40-yard killing range most of the time. When he strays too far beyond that distance, perhaps ignoring your command or signal, and flushes a bird, merely withholding your fire will also prevent him from wrapping his lips around the feathered quarry he so eagerly wants to catch and retrieve.

Since the pointing dog and the flushing dog are separate and distinct types, both in their manner of hunting and in their development, there comes a time when the generalities that apply to all bird dogs in their initial indoctrination must give way to explicit approaches tailored to each. In the chapters that immediately follow, we'll delve into detailed training procedures specifically geared to each of the two types.

CHAPTER 10

FORMAL FIELD TRAINING: POINTING DOGS

When you began contemplating acquisition of a bird dog, you carefully considered a great many aspects before deciding on the type and the breed to choose. Having chosen in favor of a pointing dog, you know basically how he hunts and how he is supposed to handle his game. But to understand how to train a pointing dog successfully for the field, you should know more about what motivates him.

Uppermost is the pointing dog's desire to search out and find birds; that compulsion should be stronger even than his instinct, once having found birds, to point. Depending on his breed and individuality, the pointing dog will range freely, sometimes casting long distances to reach promising cover, in quest of birds.

Although this impulse to seek and find birds is an inherited trait, it must be nurtured and encouraged to bring it to peak potential. If underdeveloped, it will actually slow down the training process and, worse, substantially diminish the dog's productiveness in the field. If squelched by too early and too much discipline, it can leave a dog almost totally valueless as a hunter.

Next to his intense ardor to search for game comes the pointing dog's instinctive pause at the sight and/or scent of birds. The point is really little more than the momentary pause a predatory animal takes during a stalk, just prior to pouncing on its prey. Members of the cat

171

family are prime examples. In the pointing breeds, this tendency has merely been intensified by countless generations of selective breeding. Proper training extends the point's duration, keeping the dog staunchly immobile until the gunner arrives to flush and shoot the quarry.

With the exception of the so-called versatile hunting breeds, the average traditional pointing dog does not generally exhibit a deep-seated natural fetching instinct. Many pointers and setters seem to take naturally to retrieving during their first season afield, racing out to grab a dead or crippled bird and, with some coaxing, returning it to hand. Yet, if not eventually force-trained to retrieve, some will fetch only occasionally—and sometimes not at all—in their second or third years.

A potentially promising pointing dog must display an ever-increasing desire to hunt for and locate birds; a reasonably strong inclination to point—at least momentarily—the birds he does find; some propensity for helping the hunter in the recovery of downed birds; good to excellent scenting abilities, plus sufficient tractability for the dog to respond to his owner's vocal or signaled commands to hunt to the front.

Usually, most of these criteria will begin to surface, in varying degree, as the pup attains the age of six to ten or twelve months, assuming he has been given the benefit of frequent opportunities to go afield and make contact with birds, as outlined in Chapters 6 and 9. Since a pointing dog should be encouraged to search assiduously and enthusiastically, he must be given more freedom to develop naturally. By the nature of his work he is often called upon to cover ground at fairly long distances from the gunner and, consequently, does not need to be held under the tight control required in handling a flushing dog.

Although a pointing dog may appear much easier to transform into a functional, productive bird dog than one of the flushing types, actually, a flushing breed can be turned into a productive bird dog more quickly than can a pointing breed, primarily because the flush-

---

Above:
The average traditional pointing dog does not normally display a predisposition for retrieving.

Below:
Sight points are okay for a very young pointing dog, but pointing by scent for such game birds as this bobwhite quail is what you must promote in him.

ing types can be introduced to field training under more artificially contrived circumstances, and need only be held within gun range initially, in order to help put birds in the bag.

On the other hand, the pointing dog should eventually be brought under control—if he is to hunt for and serve the gun in a practical manner—when he displays the necessary verve, drive, and desire to hunt. When that will take place, of course, is contingent upon a great number of variables, including the kind and frequency of field trips given him, his breed, breeding (inheritance), individuality, natural abilities, and early basic training. Even under the same circumstances, some breeds will develop faster than others; the variation will likely be more noticeable, though, among individuals than between different breeds.

Once he evidences the previously mentioned qualities, thereby giving notice that he's ready to be brought under more persuasive tutelage and better control, the average pointing dog is on his way toward earning his keep. Long before that time, however, you should have given serious thought to the goals you wish to set for yourself and your pointing dog. By goals, we mean the degree of "finish" you intend to put on your dog.

The minimum performance a pointing dog must be capable of, if he's going to help put any birds in your game pocket, includes:

    (1) Hunting boldly and with enthusiasm;
    (2) Covering his ground intelligently, seeking birdy objectives;
    (3) Taking some directions by hand, voice, and whistle;
    (4) Pointing staunchly;
    (5) "Pointing dead" in lieu of retrieving birds to hand.

On the other hand, should you wish to produce what is generally regarded as a fully finished pointing dog, you'll have to add to the list the refinements of:

    (1) Being steady to wing and shot;
    (2) Honoring another dog's point;
    (3) Retrieving to hand.

There are lots of good reasons why some men settle for less than a fully finished pointing dog, including limitations of time and suitable facilities, as well as a shortage of wild birds. Then, too, some sportsmen simply do not feel they need to polish a dog to the nth degree, as long as he produces enough birds to keep their sport interesting and fruitful.

Conversely, many men would consider that they had done only half a job unless their dogs were brought to the level of fully finished performance. Certainly, little quarrel can be found with the end result of seeing a perfectly mannered pointing dog demonstrate the highest quality of his art. Whichever way you choose to go will, of course, be your own decision. Here, however, we intend to examine all the aspects involved in training the pointing dog to full polish.

Assuming you've followed the training suggestions already discussed in earlier chapters, your pup should have learned much of what constitutes his basic education. Most of the material explored has had application to both types and any breed of bird dog, the few exceptions having been specifically noted. In order to avoid needless repetition, we'll skip detailed directions for teaching lessons already described and, instead, provide additional explanation of those aspects that most directly affect the pointing dog and influence his development.

During all those preliminary field trips with your pointing breed pup, you were encouraging his innate hunting desire and acquainting him with a natural pattern of hunting, as well as introducing the noise of the gun. Simultaneously, you were able to familiarize him with, and increasingly obtain obedience to, the ''Whoa'' command, both by voice and whistle. You also should have elicited from him the proper response to the recall or ''Here'' directive and taught him the meaning of the spoken ''All Right'' and ''Go On'' orders, along with their two-toot whistle equivalents.

You've given him a pretty free rein in the field so as not to curb his growing desire to search actively for and find birds. On later outings, you've been able to fire a blank while he was busy chasing a bird or otherwise preoccupied. He has flash pointed both sparrows and game birds, and during open season you've managed to kill at least a few birds for him. You know you have the makings of a good bird dog. What he now needs is the sort of work that will progressively direct his efforts into more productive results for the gun, while retaining as much of his fire and stylishness as possible.

If your supply of wild birds is abundant and your open season long, you'll be able to provide him with the kind of work that is tough to equal. However, if your situation is typical of the average hunter's, you will have to resort to planted birds—either your own or those purchased from a commercial shooting preserve. In any event, you will have to concentrate principally on the following aspects:

PROMOTING STAUNCHNESS ON POINT

Except for an insatiable appetite for searching, the most important part of a pointing dog's job is his naturally strong instinct to point the birds he's found. In the young dog the inborn proclivity to point manifests itself very early, in what are commonly called "sight points," momentary rigid stances assumed on objects or creatures that move enticingly. These run the gamut from butterflies and grasshoppers to frogs and beetles—the nonsinging kind, of course.

Sight points are, at best, of limited training value, proving only that a puppy may be imbued with normal pointing instinct and that he may possess a stylish pointing attitude. Such sight points can be encouraged by employing a bird wing, a few feathers tied together, or even a piece of cloth, on the end of a string or length of monofilament attached to a stick or fishing rod, which is manipulated tantilizingly in front of a pointing breed pup. Most puppies will instinctively chase and try to catch the moving object.

Each time the pup gets close to the wing or feathers, you should jerk the "bird" out of his reach. Soon, tiring of chasing and realizing that pursuit is futile, the pup usually will begin stalking the object and, as he approaches closely, point it. When he does, you can try touching him, stroking him along the back, and running your hand from the base of his tail upwards toward the tip. Surprisingly, even the youngest pointing dog often will exhibit both staunchness and high style in these elementary sight points.

However, what you really wish to promote in your young dog is his instinct to point staunchly the *scent* of game birds. During his prehunting season outings, if he finds and flash points a game bird, you should attempt to get to him as quickly but as unexcitedly as possible. Stifle your impulse to talk to him the first couple of times—conversation will only serve to break the mesmerizing effect of the moment—and, instead, try to get your hands on him. You may get close any number of times only to have him break and chase just before touching him. Don't let that discourage you; sooner or later he'll hold his point long enough for you to put your hands on him.

When that occurs, run one hand gently down his chest and the other soothingly along his back and flanks, telling him in a low, almost whispered tone to "Whoa." If possible, elevate his tail by lightly palming it in an upward direction. At the same time, nudge his hindquarters forward ever so slightly, pushing him toward the bird. If he is ready to be staunched, he'll resist this forward motion and stiffen even more rigidly. When you first experience this resistance in him, don't press your luck too far. One or two gentle nudges are enough before releasing him with a tap on the head and an "All Right, Go On" command, as you both move in to flush the bird.

The more you can handle your young dog when he's on point, the stauncher he generally will become. If you regularly reach his side and stroke and style him on point, he will come to enjoy pointing. Not only does the tantalizing aroma of bird scent filling his nostrils turn him on, but knowing that he's the center of your attention gives him keen pleasure. By gradually increasing the duration of his points before moving in to flush the bird, you'll soon have your dog standing game staunchly.

During the public open hunting season, or on commercial shooting preserves, killing birds over your dog will further promote staunchness, if you shoot only at those he points solidly. It may be a temptation to take a crack at a bird he bumps, either deliberately or accidentally, but you'll only encourage him to continue bumping (flushing) if you do so. By using some self-discipline and holding your fire, you'll help your dog to learn by association that the only birds you're interested in are those he points staunchly.

Most pointing breed pups can be depended upon to point with reasonable staunchness after a single full season's experience. By that, we mean holding a point long enough for the gunner to come abreast of them before they break, flush, and chase. For the individual dogs that show little or no desire to hold point more than a few seconds, even after innumerable contacts with game birds, work on a check cord is an absolute necessity. (How to deal with this problem and other frequently encountered dilemmas will be discussed in detail in Chapter 12.)

DEVELOPING HUNTING PATTERN

A pointing dog's hunting pattern has long been a subject for debate. One faction prefers and strongly defends the methodical quartering, or what is called the "windshield wiper," pattern. Simply described, it finds the dog working the cover in front of the gun from right to left and then vice versa, never failing to make his turns to the front—away from the gunner—at a more or less constant range.

Many bird hunters prefer a less mechanical ground pattern in their pointing dogs, favoring one that permits more latitude and encourages a search borne of birdwise experience. This makes a dog more interesting to hunt with and, after acquiring the wisdom of a few seasons, perhaps more productive than his methodical patterning counterpart.

As already described, in his early outings you began subliminally developing in your pup the staying out front habit by changing your direction each time he changed his. A bit later, you called his name, 177 waved your arm, and blew the two-blast whistle signal to indicate that you wanted him to take a new tack. If he learned to follow your directions reasonably well, you should have had little difficulty in shaping a functional ground pattern in him by adopting a zigzag course of hunting yourself.

However, if he's been consistently ignoring your directional change signals, you will have no alternative but to snap a 50-foot check cord on him and drill him in a mechanical manner. Every time

Below:
Stimulating staunchness on point is demonstrated in this sequence by professional trainer Ed Frisella of Peace Dale, R.I. Here a young German shorthaired pointer finds a planted quail.
Opposite, above:
Immediately he goes on point, while Ed, holding check cord, cautions the pup softly to ''Whoa.''
Opposite, below:
Coming up slowly, Ed gets his hands on the pup. Stroking him soothingly, he styles the pup and, simultaneously, nudges his hindquarters forward, pushing him toward the bird. The dog resists flushing the bird and stiffens, becoming stauncher on point.

he reaches the end of the cord, call his name, wave your arm, and double toot him as you jerk the cord, which will make him realize he's under your control and must obey. After a few such sessions, try him again without the check cord. Should he backslide, just snap on the cord again.

All but the most recalcitrant dogs generally will respond well to this training. Make sure, though, that you have not been overdoing your whistle directions in the first place, before you start such check cord work.

ESTABLISHING PROPER NATURAL RANGE

The species of game birds you hunt, the type of terrain and cover they inhabit, and the breed of pointing dog you have chosen will determine how far your dog should range. Obviously, if you've chosen an English pointer, say, for big-country bobwhite hunting, you don't expect a close-ranging dog. Yet, for any number of reasons, you may want your dog to adjust his range to some extent.

Hunting pattern sometimes has to be taught in a mechanical manner at the end of a 50-foot check cord.

Certainly, before you can determine that, you'll have to have a pretty good idea of just what your dog's natural range is, something you can discover only after having hunted with him for a while. Putting him in country most typical of the birds and terrain and cover you'll ordinarily encounter, and giving him free rein, provides the best indicator of his normal range.

Should it prove to be a bit too wide for comfortable hunting, you can try shortening it. To accomplish this in the natural manner, which is definitely preferable, work him as frequently as possible in very heavy cover, while he's still young. The denseness of the cover will force him to reduce his range as will the necessity of keeping track of you.

Another method of trimming his range naturally is to work him where birds are superabundant, which usually means on a commercial shooting preserve. Released bobwhite or Coturnix quail are ideal birds to use for encouraging a pointing dog to hunt closer to the gun. For the dog that is really hunting, and not just running, the incentive of finding large numbers of birds in closer proximity to his owner will generally shorten him up in five or six trips.

Although a dog's natural range can be reduced somewhat, it is practically impossible to widen it. Of course, there are some field trial type dogs that are "pushed" to their limits, or beyond, by trainers handling exclusively from horseback but these dogs are seldom hunting in earnest; rather, they are simply running as wide as they can to keep away from and ahead of their handlers.

Aside from shortening a dog's range in a natural manner, there are a few artificial means you can try, which will be examined and described in Chapter 12.

STEADY TO WING AND SHOT

Requiring that a pointing dog be steady to wing and shot—which simply means remaining immobile at the bird's flush and the gunner's shot, until ordered to fetch or in the event of a miss to resume hunting—has always been a source of controversy. Some hunters label such training as totally unnecessary, an affectation reserved only for field trial performers.

Another group believes that a dog should be steady to wing, but not to shot, contending that shot-breaking enables a dog to get the jump on a bird that may be grounded but not down for the count and thereby save the cripple for the bag. Field trial competitors have no choice; their dogs must be steady to both wing and shot.

There can be little doubt that the pointing dog that remains steady to wing and shot epitomizes the ultimate in class, exhibiting the polished manners of a fully trained bird dog under complete control of his handler. In addition to the aesthetics involved, such performance does have some practical value. For example, the dog that breaks wing may go charging along right under a low-flying bird, causing the hunter to risk hitting the dog if he shoots. The shot-breaker, intent on getting to the downed bird as fast as possible, can easily run right over and flush another bird or, worse yet, a whole bevy, leaving the gunner standing there with egg on his face. Thus,

---

Opposite, above:
Steadiness to wing (and to shot, which is simply a repetition of the same basic procedure) is shown in this series, again by professional trainer Ed Frisella, using an English pointer. With dog on check cord, Ed admonishes "Whoa."
Opposite, below:
He staunches the pointer, picking him up by the root of his tail, as assistant (not pictured) prepares to flush bobwhite quail.
Below:
At flush, Ed lets dog hit slack check cord and hollers "Whoa,"
pulling dog back into original pointing position.

there are some distinct advantages to having a completely steady pointing dog.

You will have to weigh the pros and cons and then decide how far you want to take your pointing dog, part way or all the way—or not at all—along the road to steadiness. Should you opt to train him to be steady, you'll have to start first on keeping him immobile at the flush. To do this, you'll need two things, a check cord and a helper.

If your dog is reliably staunch on point, permit him to run without dragging the check cord. Should you have any doubts, it's safer to snap the cord on him before turning him loose to work on a pigeon or quail you've planted for him. Hunt him into the wind, toward the bird, but whatever you do, don't make it too easy or mechanical by leading him right to it.

When your dog finds and points the bird, get to him as rapidly as you can without rushing or appearing to be flustered or excited. The calmer you are, the more likely your dog is to reflect the same attitude and thus remain rock staunch on point. Get hold of the check cord if he's dragging it, or snap it on his collar if he's not, all the while talking softly, reassuringly, to keep him standing his bird solidly.

Signal your assistant to flush the bird, making sure he forces it to fly away from and not back toward the dog. Since it's highly probable that your dog will break and chase, as he has been doing previously, keep a firm hold with your gloved hands on the end of the check cord. Just as he's used up almost all the cord's slack, brace yourself and command him, "Whoa" in a loud, sharp, decisive voice. If he's been obeying this command with alacrity, he should stop right in his tracks; if he hasn't and doesn't, he'll hit the end of the cord going full tilt and, doubtless, swap ends.

Either way, go to your dog and carry him in both arms or walk him back by the collar to the exact spot where he first pointed the bird. Set him up again on point, tell him "Whoa" in a crisp tone, and style him in a proper stance, keeping him there, stroking and talking soothingly to him for at least a full minute. Then tap him lightly on the head and give him the two-blast whistle signal to continue hunting.

During this process—which can be agonizingly slow with some dogs or amazingly fast with others—do not shoot over your dog. Once he's demonstrated that he's fully steady to wing, on and off the check cord, you can kill a few birds for him, letting him break shot to retrieve if he is doing that, or "point dead," if you *don't* plan to make him steady to shot. It's advisable to deliberately miss a bird

184

Ed Frisella teaches this English pointer to stop to flush. After the dog broke to a flushed bird, Ed brought him back to the place where he should have stopped and sets him up once again on point, commanding "Whoa."

once in a while and "Whoa" the dog after he takes a few bounds in the direction the bird flew. After all, you don't want him needlessly using up time and energy chasing birds you've missed.

Once you've steadied your dog to wing, never shoot at any bird if the dog breaks at the flush. To do so, of course, will only encourage him to commit the same transgression again. Instead, go to the dog and carry or walk him back to the place from which he broke; set him up on point and follow the same procedure you used to steady him originally.

If you plan to train your dog to be steady to shot as well as to wing, you'll have to backtrack a bit in the aforementioned routine. When your dog evidences that he's completely steady to wing, he'll be ready to begin shooting over, using only .22 blanks, whenever your helper flushes a bird the dog has pointed and handled properly.

Again, you'll need the check cord. When the dog establishes point, walk up to him and either snap it onto his collar or, if he's trailing it, take hold of the cord. Have your assistant flush the bird; your dog will remain steady to wing. As the bird gets well underway, your helper should fire his .22 blank gun. With the crack of the gun, your dog will attempt to break shot. Prevent him from doing so by restraining him with tension on the cord and giving him a crisply commanding "Whoa."

If he stands steady at your command, having taken only a step or two, go to him, style him up, and tell him what a fine dog he is. However, should he ignore your order and really burst out after the bird, let him "run out the string," give him a loud "Whoa," and up end him. Then go get him, carrying or walking him back to his original position and setting him up again on point while you tell him a bit about what "Whoa" means.

Gradually, your dog should learn to remain steady to shot. When he demonstrates his reliability, change over from the .22 blank pistol to a 20-gauge shotgun, continuing to have your helper do the flushing and the shooting. After a few successful sessions with the 20 gauge, you should test your dog's steadiness by having your assistant kill a bird that the dog has pointed.

If it's your lucky day, your dog won't budge an inch at the flush, the shot, and the fall. Count your blessings and resolve to go to church or synagogue twice next weekend as you "Whoa" your dog in a confident voice. While you keep him standing pat, butter him up with all the kind words you can muster. Meanwhile, have your helper saunter out unexcitedly, pick up the dead bird, and bring it back to your dog. Permit your dog to sniff and mouth the bird for a minute or two, keeping him standing in the same place until you give the order to start hunting again.

By letting the dog get his mouth on the bird, you'll be fostering in him the idea that he'll never be denied his reward when he remains

---

Above:
Training your dog to back requires the availability of a reliably staunch pointing dog and a planted game bird that will stay put. In this sequence, Ed Frisella brings the pupil on check cord to the point of a veteran English setter.
Center:
When he's certain the student sees the other dog on point, Ed commands "Whoa" and makes it stick.
Below:
With constant repetition, the pupil has learned to back the veteran on sight.

steady to wing and shot. The quicker he forms this mental association, the sooner he'll become dependably steady. You should, therefore, continue having your helper retrieve every dead bird for the
dog until he has reached such reliability that you can do the flushing
and shooting yourself.

Since every dog is an individual, it isn't possible to set forth a rigid
schedule as to when you should attempt to steady your dog to wing
and shot. Those dogs that progress very rapidly and are provided
with far more than average opportunities to work on game birds may
begin steadying by the end of their first season. With sensitive dogs
that do not get too much bird work, it is sometimes best to wait
almost another full season before attempting to steady them. You
will have to use your own intimate knowledge of your dog's character and responsiveness, plus a bit of discretion, to determine precisely the proper timing for starting this training.

Teaching the pointing dog to remain steady to wing and shot without taking away from him any of his innate verve, dash, and style is
the mark of a truly adroit and sensitive trainer. Perhaps the most
important thing to keep in mind is making certain your dog is ready
for such lessons and then administering them with patient
perseverance.

STOPPING TO FLUSH

Even if you have chosen not to train your pointing dog to be steady
to shot, but only to wing, he should be taught to stop to flush, which
means that your dog will halt and remain immobile whenever a bird
flushes in his vicinity. Oftentimes, especially on gusty days, game
birds will be unusually spooky. Then, too, on certain days scenting
conditions may be bad. At such times your dog might inadvertently
bump a bird, through no real fault of his own. If this is the case, and
your dog stops to flush, it is permissible to shoot the wild flushing
bird. But if your dog deliberately crowds a bird into flying and then
stops at the flush, you should not shoot, because the dog has made a
willful error.

Teaching your dog to stop to flush is relatively easy. Every time a
bird gets airborne anywhere near your dog, for whatever the reason,
command "Whoa" and make it stick. Should the dog fail to heed
your order, go get him and—just as you did in training him to be
staunch and/or steady—return him to the spot where he should have
stopped, set him up and repeat the command to whoa while you
make him stand for a moment or two.

188

Left:
The first step in force training your dog to retrieve is to command
"Fetch," preceded by his name, and pop the dummy into his mouth.
Closing his mouth, tell him "Hold." Photo by Jerome Knap.
Right:
Next, you'll have to get your dog to open his mouth and reach out
for the dummy as you order him to "Fetch." Ear pinching is
necessary. Photo by Jerome Knap.

As in most other aspects of training, consistency and constant repetition are the keys to success in teaching your dog to stop to flush. Obviously, the task will be much simpler if you've already trained him to be steady to wing. If he's been taught to be steady to shot as well, then he should not move after the flush and the shot until you tell him to "Go On."

HONORING THE POINT

Another prime example of what some hunters consider field trial frivolousness is training a pointing dog to honor another dog's point. Honoring, or backing, as it is often called, means only that one dog, upon sighting another dog on point, will stop and remain immobile, just as staunchly as if he himself had found and nailed down a bird. It   189 matters not at all whether the honoring dog has scented game; even if the wind is right for him and he knows the other dog is pointing old scent, he must be trained to acknowledge, or honor, on sight the other dog's "find."

To do otherwise could result in a flushed bird, assuming the second dog was approaching upwind of the dog already on point. Failure to honor sometimes leads to one dog attempting to steal another dog's point, creeping in jealously and crowding a bird into flight before the gun arrives within shooting range.

If you hunt your pointing dog with a friend's, you'll find it highly practicable to teach both dogs to back on sight, or at least on command. Without such training, a brace of pointing dogs hunting together can produce a nightmare of bumped birds and hackle-raising altercations between both dogs and humans.

Training your dog to back requires the availability of a good reliably staunch pointing dog and, usually, a planted game bird that will stay put. If you don't have a hunting buddy who owns such a dog, your best bet will be to solicit the aid of a commercial shooting preserve owner or manager with an experienced pointing dog that will stand game like the Rock of Gibraltar.

Get the veteran dog on point and then work yours, on a check cord, into position where he can easily see the first dog on point from a reasonable distance. When you're certain your dog spots the other dog pointing, tell him to "Whoa" and make sure he obeys the command instantly. Assuming he does stop right in his tracks, go to him and, soothingly stroking and styling him, keep him standing fast for a minute or two before having your friend or whoever is helping you flush and shoot the bird.

Should your dog indicate an unwillingness to point upon sighting the other dog standing fast, bring him in closer, working downwind so plenty of scent reaches his nose and he wants to point the bird instinctively. Just make sure, though, that he freezes a few feet behind or to the side of the dog that has made the find. Once your dog seems to catch on to the fact that he must stop at the sight of another dog on point, lead him in only on the upwind side where no scent can reach him. Repetition should eventually condition him to freeze instantly whenever he spies another dog on point.

TRAINING TO RETRIEVE

As noted earlier, many pointing breeds are not imbued with a particularly strong retrieving instinct. For this reason, some hunters shun all fetch training of their pointers and, instead, merely encourage them to "point dead," an act that is self-explanatory. Others attempt to stimulate whatever natural fetching proclivities their dogs may possess and settle for having their birds retrieved part-time or part-way, strictly at the dogs' whims.

Although the natural method of teaching retrieving—which is the one most commonly employed with spaniels and retrieving breeds—is very simple, with many pointing dogs it has the disadvantage cited above. In addition, dogs educated in fetching the natural way often refuse even to touch various game birds, woodcock being the most universally rejected.

Thus, if you really want your pointing dog to become a full-time, completely reliable retriever of the upland birds you shoot, you will have no choice but to force train him to retrieve. This involves a lengthy series of lessons that you should not attempt until he is pointing staunchly, has an unquenchable love of bird hunting, been steadied to wing and/or shot, and taught to stop to flush—if these latter refinements are included in your training plans.

A course in force training to retrieve is usually slow and monotonous both for dog and trainer. Its basic purpose is to make a dog fetch, not because he wants to but because he is ordered to. Since strict discipline and stern methods must be used to elicit prompt obedience, judicious care must be exercised so as not to impair the dog's spirit and eagerness. However, once the lessons are begun, they should be brought to successful conclusion; otherwise, it's a fair certainty the dog will give up all semblance of interest in fetching birds in the future.

If you are not always in complete control of your temper, if you're inclined to become impatient or easily discouraged, if you're unable to spare ten minutes daily, then you should think twice about undertaking the task of force training your dog to retrieve. Be as objective as possible when making this decision. Should your decision be negative, either teach your dog to "point dead" or invest a few dollars in having him professionally taught to retrieve. If your response is affirmative, then proceed as follows.

The equipment you'll need consists of a choke collar, either leather or chain, a 6- or 8-foot leash, a 25-foot check cord, and a retrieving dummy. The dummy can be store bought or a do-it-yourself piece of handiwork, usually a square of burlap rolled tightly around a ¾-inch-diameter dowel and fastened firmly to it with a couple of wrappings of fine wire. The overall diameter of the dummy should not exceed 2¼ inches and its length not more than 10 inches.   191

Adding a few drops of commercial scent of the principal game bird you hunt to the dummy will make it more appealing to your dog.

With the choke collar and leash on your dog, take him to a quiet, distraction-free area and try to interest him in the sight and smell of the dummy. Tease him a bit with it; arouse his curiosity and then let him play with it for a few minutes. When he seems familiar with the dummy, take it from him by commanding "Give," and, if necessary, squeezing his lips gently against his teeth until he relinquishes the dummy.

Put your dog in the sitting position, and open his mouth with your left hand (the same pressure on his lips against his teeth will accomplish this). Command "Fetch," preceded by his name, and pop the dummy into his mouth. Make sure his lips are not jammed between his teeth and the dummy, then close his mouth and tell him "Hold." Repeat the hold order every time he tries to get rid of the dummy, simultaneously clamping your hand over his upper and lower jaws to keep it in his mouth. Try to keep him holding the dummy for about fifteen or twenty seconds, then order him to "Give," and *take* it from him; do not let him spit it out.

Repeat the entire sequence about half-a-dozen times each day until your dog is holding the dummy without attempting to drop it. If he tries to spit it out, use a steady upward pull on the leash to tighten the choke collar until he holds the dummy securely. When he holds correctly and relinquishes at your "Give" command, pat and praise him profusely.

After you're certain he'll hold the dummy, move off a very short distance and order him to "Fetch, here." Should he drop the dummy in his eagerness to get to you, pick it up, take him back to his original sitting position, command "Fetch" and, as you place the dummy in his mouth, "Hold." Walk away again and, cautioning him to "Hold," tell him once more, "Fetch, here." Continue this, spending no more than ten minutes at it daily, for however many days it requires to achieve perfection.

Once your dog is holding the dummy firmly and bringing it a short distance to you on the "Fetch, here" command, have him walk at heel while carrying the dummy. For some reason, most dogs take pride in this act and will be perfectly content to strut along at your side with the dummy for as long as four or five minutes.

Moving on to the next phase, you'll have to teach your dog to open his mouth and reach out for the dummy when you tell him to "Fetch." At this juncture, in 99 cases out of 100, some force must be used; conventionally, it consists of ear-pinching, something that

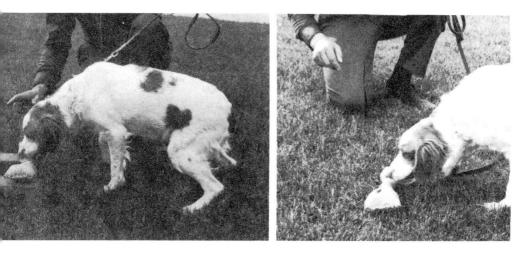

Left:
Getting your dog to pick the dummy up off the ground is more easily accomplished by laying the dummy, in bridgelike fashion, across a pair of bricks. Photo by Jerome Knap.
Right:
The last phase is teaching your dog to pick the dummy up right off the ground at your order to "Fetch." Photo by Jerome Knap.

sounds cruel. Actually, it causes the dog no more than mild discomfort, just enough to make him open his mouth in protest, at which point you quickly slip in the dummy and order "Fetch," followed by "Hold." Immediately after he has the dummy in his mouth, release the pressure of your thumbnail and forefinger on his ear.

Don't forget to let him know what a good boy he is when he reaches for and holds the dummy on your command. Eventually, as you gradually make him reach out farther—as much as a foot or so—to receive the dummy, begin lowering it toward the ground. If your progress has been slow and steady, he shouldn't balk at having to reach down as well as forward. At the first refusal, go back again to the ear-pinch and make him accept the dummy. Remember, this is slow, sometimes agonizing, training, but only patience and perseverance pay dividends. Never permit backsliding.

The next job is to have your dog make his pick up of the dummy off the ground. There are several methods of approaching this. The one we favor takes a little longer than most others, but it also requires less gruff force. Place a pair of bricks broadside down on the ground, leaving roughly half a foot of space between them. Lay your dummy, in bridgelike fashion, across the bricks. Now, lead your dog right up to the dummy and tell him to "Fetch." Chances are he won't obey the order. While pinching his ear, push his head down toward the dummy and don't relinquish either pressure until he takes it in his mouth. Then make him hold, or even carry while walking at heel, for a minute or two before commanding him to "Give." Repeat this four or five times at each session.

After your dog consistently makes the pick up on the "Fetch" command alone, without the need for force, start whoaing him a few feet away from the dummy resting on the bricks and order him to retrieve. Work regularly on this and, as he complies properly, stop him progressively farther away from the dummy. When you're asking him to go forward more than 5 or 6 feet, you'll have to switch from the leash to a check cord. This will enable you to pull him in to you if he picks up the dummy but doesn't want to return with it. Your goal at this stage is to have your dog dependably retrieving on command from as far away as 15 or 20 feet, at first with the check cord but eventually without it.

Picking the dummy up right off the ground is the last phase of teaching your dog to retrieve by the force-training method. Usually, if you've progressed successfully to this point, using the procedure outlined, you won't experience much difficulty. However, if you do, merely take him on lead or cord over to the dummy and push his head down, simultaneously pinching his ear just as you did in earlier lessons. A few such sessions will generally prove to be sufficient in having him pick up the dummy on the ground. Once again, gradually increase the distance of his retrieves on the check cord and when he's performing well, remove the cord while working him.

Now, you should begin tossing the dummy for him to retrieve, keeping him at "Whoa" until you tell him by name, "Fetch." Once he's complying nicely, you can begin varying both the locale and the type of dummy for his retrieving practice. It will prove helpful to you to read the following chapter which, although focusing on flushing dogs, includes additional details on retrieving.

If you and your pointing dog have come this far with reasonable success, you've both done well. There may be some problems, though, and you may be confused about how to deal with them. The most common of these are discussed in Chapter 12.

CHAPTER 11

FORMAL FIELD TRAINING: FLUSHING DOGS

If you've selected a flushing dog as the type best suited to your personal requirements, you have a great deal of real pleasure ahead of you. Whichever breed you've chosen, his training and performance should be based on the standards that make up the job description of the Springer spaniel. Historically, the spaniel is the number-one flushing dog in the uplands and thus sets the standard for all flushing breeds to follow.

Foremost of the spaniel's instincts is a strong inclination to hunt for, find, and vigorously flush game birds for the gun. Yet, despite his centuries-old inheritance, this urge, like most instincts, must be awakened and cultivated by proper stimulation.

Second is the spaniel's natural enthusiasm for retrieving, something most field-bred members of the breed are highly adept at doing. Often, however, the desire to retrieve can easily be overshadowed by the spaniel's keener desire to search for and flush birds. The opposite is generally true of the retriever breeds; they customarily require far more encouragement to spark their desire to hunt ahead of the gun than to retrieve.

Basically, the ideal flushing dog should evidence a growing zeal for hunting birds and a willingness to search diligently at all times. He should demonstrate that he has a good nose and is learning how to   195 use it; that he bores in boldly, decisively, and gets his bird airborne without hesitation. He should show confidence in his manner and intelligence in his quartering while exhibiting prompt obedience to his owner's commands by voice, hand, and whistle. He must hunt inside effective shotgun range and, on command, should quickly retrieve with tender mouth all dead or crippled birds.

Generally, if your pup has been accorded the early training and field experience detailed in Chapters 6 and 9, he should already have a good start on what is expected of him. As mentioned in the previous chapter on formal training of the pointing breeds, most of the material examined in the early portions of this book is equally applicable to both types and any breed of bird dog, the several exceptions having been specifically noted. As before, detailed instructions for lessons already described are not repeated here; rather, supplementary explanation will be offered of those aspects that most directly affect the flushing dog and influence his successful development.

Concurrent with his preliminary field trips, on which you were promoting your pup's desire to hunt and chase birds of all kinds, you were also teaching him to use his naturally strong instincts to retrieve every time he picked up and carried a tossed dummy. After a while, when you moved these informal retrieving sessions outdoors and your pup was eagerly fetching your makeshift dummy, you judiciously conditioned him to the low-level sound of simulated gunfire. Simultaneously, you saw to it that your flushing dog was consistently obeying the "Hup" or "Sit" command on voice, hand, and whistle signal. You also made sure he was well schooled in the recall order, as well as the "All Right" and "Go On" commands, both by voice and whistle. During all this time, you were advancing your pup's natural retrieving capabilities. Let's take a detailed look at how that should be done.

NATURAL RETRIEVING

After moving your retrieving sessions outdoors, where you began shooting a cap gun, you can start substituting a regular dummy for the sock, handkerchief, or glove you used to get your pup initiated to fetching. This can be one of the kapok-filled canvas kind or a homemade dummy of burlap rolled tightly around a ¾-inch-diameter dowel, approximately 10 inches long, and secured with fine wire or strong rubber bands. Sprinkling it with several drops of commercial scent of the principal game bird you intend to hunt will perk up your dog's interest and also accustom him to that scent.

Gradually, as your pup progresses, you should lengthen the distance you toss the dummy. If the pup shows any hesitation about returning with it, put a check cord on him and, after calling his name followed by the order "Fetch, here," pull him in to you, gently but inexorably. Then command him to "Hup," or "Sit," and take the dummy from him as you tell him to "Give."

By the time he's well conditioned to the noise of the cap pistol going off every time the dummy is thrown for him to fetch, you can switch over to the .22 caliber blank gun. If you suspect the noise will bother him, have a helper—wives or teen-age children make very good ones—stand off about 25 yards, fire the blank, and chuck the dummy as high in the air as possible.

The pup, sitting at your side, should be attracted by the gunfire and the airborne dummy. Tell him in excited tones to "Fetch," and double toot your whistle. Unless he's extremely atypical, the sound of the blank going off some distance away won't faze him in the least, and he'll already be racing to retrieve the dummy even before your order. Never fail to pet and praise him when he returns to you with the dummy.

Repeat the procedure three or four more times, having your assistant move a few yards closer to you and the dog for each shot and toss, as long as your dog shows no nervousness over the noise. After several similar training periods with your helper edging nearer and nearer, you should be able to take over the shooting and throwing chores yourself. Watch carefully, though, for any adverse reactions; if any are detected, return to using a helper who shoots farther away from the dog.

All these retrieving sessions should be increasing your dog's enthusiasm for fetching in a natural, eager manner. His progress and experience will be further enhanced if you attach a number of pigeon or game bird wings to your dummy. These can either be taped on or secured by heavy rubber bands. The wing-equipped dummies will begin conditioning your dog to the feel and taste of feathers before you actually have him retrieve any dead birds.

Assuming his progress is normal—and don't forget that you shouldn't be guilty of extremes, either in pushing him too fast or in giving him too little training—providing him with the chance to fetch some real birds is your next step. If you can afford them, and have a commercial shooting preserve nearby, using bobwhite quail or chukar partridges will prove to be more realistic than using pigeons. However, pigeons are generally easier to get, as well as being considerably less expensive.

197

Whichever bird you utilize, wring its neck so as to dispatch it quickly, mercifully, and without having it bleed. With your dog sitting at your side, fire your .22 blank gun—remembering to hold it behind you at arm's length—and chuck the bird 15 or 20 feet as you order your dog, by name, to "Fetch," accompanying the verbal command with the "All Right" whistle signal. Even though this warm, heavily feathered object is new to him (remember, this is taking place before the public open hunting season), the chances are good that he'll pick it up with minimal hesitation and deliver it to your hand.

When he brings in the bird, gush over his good work and let him hold the bird a moment or two, as a sort of reward. When you finally take delivery, make sure to remove any loose feathers from your dog's mouth and then chuck the bird out and have him retrieve it again. Go through the same act two or three times and quit while the dog is still eager and happy.

Intersperse the use of dead game birds—nothing larger than a chukar, though—with the plain and feather-wrapped dummies for all of your young dog's subsequent retrieving practice. This will vary the objects to be fetched and keep the dog's interest keen. Obviously, it also will condition him to retrieving whatever you ask him to fetch.

If possible, before the public hunting season for upland birds opens, allow your flushing dog to get in some practice retrieving a few birds that are shot in his presence. Since this may be his initial exposure to the sound of a shotgun, everything must be handled exactly right. What you need is a crack-shot assistant armed with a 20-gauge shotgun plus a bag of live birds, either bobwhites, chukars, or pigeons. Five or six will be enough for one go-round.

Ask your helper-gunner to station himself about 50 yards off to one side of you and your dog. Then have him throw a single bird into the air, directing it as much as is possible on a cross-quartering flight to the front, and kill it cleanly. Order your dog to fetch, and pile on the praise when he brings the bird back. Use up your remaining birds, having your dog retrieve each one.

Besides continuing to condition your flushing dog to the sound of gunfire and providing him with additional retrieving practice, the foregoing lesson gives him excellent experience in marking the fall of a bird. In the event you have several opportunities to have a few game birds or pigeons shot for your dog prior to hunting season, try picking a spot where the cover is fairly heavy. Even if he's a good marker, this will inevitably make him use his nose to find some of the dead birds.

Left:
When your flushing dog has become adept at retrieving a sock,
glove, or handkerchief, switch to a regular dummy. Photo by
Robert Elman.
Right:
Gradually lengthen the distance you toss the dummy.

Should he experience some difficulty locating a fall, go out to him and encourage him with the word "Dead," followed by an excitedly intoned "Find the Bird" and a two-toot whistle signal. Even if you know exactly where the bird is, urge your dog to seek it out himself. If he gets too far off course, call him back and, if necessary, practically lead him onto the bird, but let him find and retrieve it.

Bear in mind that, unlike the force-training system, which makes a dog retrieve whether he wants to or not, the natural method we've been describing for flushing dogs employs no pressure tactics. 199 Rather, it seeks to take advantage of the dog's naturally strong inclination to pick up and carry thrown objects, by making the act of fetching a pleasant, thoroughly enjoyable pastime. In fact, the most successful trainer is the one who psyches his fledgling pupil into believing that retrieving is not only the dog's own idea, but that it is also being done only for his pleasure.

DEVELOPING HUNTING PATTERN AND STAYING WITHIN GUN RANGE

Unlike the pointing dog that is relatively unencumbered by restrictions in his ground pattern and natural hunting range, the flushing dog, to be of any practical value, must hunt within shotgun range of his owner. The precise methodical quartering that conventionally would be frowned upon as being too mechanical in a pointer is exactly the kind of pattern the flushing dog should be trained to follow. Once the rudiments of quartering have been successfully ingrained—usually after a couple of season's experience—the flushing dog should be permitted occasionally to deviate from this methodical pattern in order to investigate birdy objectives he might otherwise have to miss.

Of course, you started conditioning your pup in developing the correct hunting pattern during his initial field trips. If your early groundwork has been properly laid, he should be eagerly hunting and quartering out front and to the sides, both naturally as well as on your voice, whistle, and hand signals. Until he has demonstrated his

---

Above:
If your dog is reluctant to return with the dummy, put a check cord on him and, ordering "Fetch, here," pull him in to you gently but inexorably. Photo by Robert Elman.
Center, left:
Don't be in a hurry to take the dummy from him, but always pet and praise him profusely when he returns it to you. Photo by Leonard Lee Rue III.
Center, right:
Encourage your young dog to enjoy retrieving, whether game birds or dummies, by having him fetch and walk at heel carrying for several minutes at a time.
Below:
In establishing ground pattern, if your flushing dog fails to turn on your order, "Hup" him with a single sharp whistle blast. Keep him sitting for half a minute, then repeat the original directional change.

unquenchable zest for seeking birds, for finding and chasing them enthusiastically, you must be careful not to dampen his ardor by applying control too soon or too strictly. Yet one of the things your flushing dog must learn within reasonable time is to hunt inside effective gun range.

You have already gotten a head start on teaching this by effecting in him a good hunting pattern. But you'll have to stay alert and keep at him regularly each time he reaches the outermost limits of shotgun range. As he swings to the left and gets out to about 35 yards, turn him to the right with your voice, the two-toot whistle blast, and the arm signal. Similarly, when he angles right and reaches approximately 35 yards, repeat the whole sequence, swinging him over to the left.

Should he fail to turn on your order, either continuing his cast beyond 35 or 40 yards or turning only part way and heading straight out front, "Hup" him with a single, sharp whistle blast, and make it authoritative! Then, after keeping him sitting for half a minute, to let him know you're in control, repeat the original directional change command he ignored.

If he has occasional lapses, "Hup" him each time and give him the turn order again. Usually, half-a-dozen outings will convince the average flushing dog that he can hunt uninterruptedly as long as he stays within range and/or obeys your turn order. Ultimately, of course, as your dog gains the wisdom and experience of a couple of season's hunting, he'll seldom need your whistle to remind him that he's overextended his proper range.

STEADY TO WING AND SHOT

The well-trained flushing dog should be steady to wing and shot, which means that he will "Hup" or "Sit" immediately after a bird is flushed or a gun is fired, and remain in that position until told to fetch or continue hunting. It is not arguable, in our opinion, as it is when

Above:
To steady your dog to wing, put him at "Hup" in front of you and chuck the dummy over your head behind you. If the dog tries to break, you'll be in position to stop him forcibly.
Below:
When he's rock steady as you stand in front of him, change your position, moving off slightly to one side, but close enough to be able to grab him if he breaks at the toss.

considering pointing dog performance, that the unsteady flushing dog is more useful because he will save more crippled birds for the bag by getting the jump on his steady counterpart.

Certainly, any flushing dog possessed of reasonably decent scenting powers should be able to trail, find, and bring back a crippled game bird with little difficulty, even if the dog has been kept in the sitting position for a couple of minutes after the shot and the fall. It is natural for the flushing dog to be an adept trailer, for he works about as much on foot scent as he does on body scent in locating and flushing live, healthy game birds.

On the other hand, far from giving the hunter an edge in collecting birds, the wing- and shot-breaking flushing dog often can prove a detriment. Chasing merrily along beneath a grass-skimming bird makes the dog almost as good a target as the bird, and, obviously, no hunter worthy of the name would chance a shot. The result . . . an opportunity lost. And possibly more than one, since the dog, chasing with reckless abandon, could quite conceivably stumble over additional birds that would be put to flight way out of gun range.

Teaching a dog steadiness to wing and shot, as with virtually any other training lesson, requires time, patience, repetition, and perseverance. Don't expect to do it overnight. What you'll have to do is go back to the yard and the retrieving dummy. For the moment, forget the blank pistol; you'll be conditioning—restricting might be more accurate—your dog to remain in one spot until he gets an order to do something he's been doing right along at his own volition—retrieving—as soon as he sees an airborne dummy.

Put him in the "Hup" position in front of you. Command "Stay" as you chuck the dummy (one to which several game bird wings have been affixed) over your head behind you. Should your dog attempt to break, you will be in an advantageous position to stop him forcibly,

---

Above, left:
If he does break, take him and set him unceremoniously back in his original position and command sharply, "Hup."
Above, right:
With proper progress, you can reintroduce the .22 blank gun. Shoot, "Hup" him with the whistle and hand signal while you or an assistant tosses the dummy.
Below:
Should your dog prove inclined to break shot, snap the check cord on him and have an assistant restrain him as you shoot and throw the dummy. Photo by Leonard Lee Rue III.

pushing him back into his original sitting attitude as you admonish him to stay. Do not let him fetch the dummy if he has broken. Make him stay "Hupped" and go get it yourself, then repeat the act up to four times in one session.

How long it will take to get this first step solidly across to your dog is something that's hard to foretell. Some dogs will get the message after only three or four days; others require as long as two weeks of daily lessons. If you stay with it, he will learn what you want and expect of him. But, remember, do not compromise. He is not to move from his sitting position until you order him to fetch.

Opposite:
Teaching your flushing dog to take a line is easy. Put him in the sitting position and, with your left arm alongside his muzzle to indicate the direction in which you want to send him, give him the verbal "All Right" order. Photo by Jerome Knap, courtesy of Jim Irwin.
Below:
Use a crack-shot assistant to dump a few birds your dog flushes and put the finishing touches on steadying him.

When he's rock steady while you stand in front of him, you can change your position by moving slightly off to the side but still close enough to be able to lunge and grab him if he breaks at the toss. A few days of this should find him waiting obediently for your order to fetch. As he demonstrates his understanding, keep him hupped after you throw the dummy, prolonging the time between the toss and your command to retrieve for just a few seconds on each outing.

Next, you'll have to station yourself behind your sitting dog. From that spot, when you chuck the dummy over his head, you'll have to be prepared to move like lightning to get your hands on him if he breaks. If he does go and you can't stop him either with a sharp "Hup" or a single whistle blast, and you can't catch him, just let him complete the retrieve but say nothing—no praise, no petting, no harsh words. Snap a check cord on him, put him at "Hup" and "Stay," and throw the dummy again. If he tries to break once more, restrain him with the check cord, go get him, and carry him back to the spot from which he broke. Set him down rather ungently, command "Hup," and immediately blow the single whistle signal. Follow up with the order to "Stay" and repeat the dummy toss.

Your tendency probably will be to overdo, especially if things are not progressing smoothly. But keep reminding yourself that four or five retrieves per lesson should be your limit. Remember, too, that no session should end on a sour note, so have your dog do something he knows perfectly and when he's done it, reward him with a pat and a few kind words.

As your dog evidences proper response on a continual basis, vary your position, going to his far right, far left, rear, and front to chuck the dummy. You can really put him to the acid test by hupping him about 35 feet from you, then lobbing the dummy within a couple of yards of him. If he sits glued to the ground until he hears your order to retrieve, you're not finished yet, but you're certainly getting good results.

When transferring your training from the backyard into the field, start your dog hunting with the double toot on the whistle and, as he turns to quarter to the right, heave the dummy to the far right. "Hup" him with the upraised arm signal and a short whistle blast as you place yourself between the dog and the dummy, a precaution that will enable you to block him should he disregard your directive. Assuming that all goes well, have him retrieve the dummy and earn the praise he seeks and deserves. Throw the dummy again and then let him resume hunting. After about ten minutes, repeat the sequence and, a short time later, repeat it once more before quitting.

After four or five such field trips, assuming he's proven to be steady to the retrieving dummy, it's time to replace it with a dead bird, preferably a bobwhite quail or chukar partridge, but an ordinary pigeon will also suffice. Merely repeat the earlier procedure, using the dead game bird instead of the dummy, and make certain to position yourself so that you can get to your dog before he gets to the tossed bird, if he attempts to fetch prior to your order.

When he exhibits the proper progress, you should start using the .22 blank gun again, in conjunction with tossing the dead bird. Shoot a blank, "Hup" him with the whistle, and throw the bird, always putting yourself between the dog and the bird. Eventually, this lesson can be coupled with the use of live planted birds, some of which should be permitted to fly off without drawing fire. This accustoms your dog to the fact that he must be steady to wing, something he previously has related only to the feathered dummies you tossed for him. Now, however, he should make the transition very quickly as you "Hup" him with the sharp single whistle blast every time he flushes a bird.

In the ensuing sessions, while your dog is busy hunting, begin firing your blank gun occasionally, even when no bird flushes, and put the whistle to him. He must also learn that he should sit at the sound of the gun and not scoot off in wild, energy-sapping pursuit of every bird you shoot at and miss.

Using that same crack-shot assistant to dump a few birds your dog flushes will help put the finishing touches on steadying him. Instruct your helper-gunner to shoot only when your dog "Hups" at flush or on your command. If the dog remains steady to wing but breaks at the shot, do everything humanly possible to stop him, even tackling him, if necessary, to prevent his reaching the dead bird. If you can manage to collar him before he gets to the bird, haul him to the spot from which he broke and, chastizing him vocally all the way back, plop him down with a forceful "Hup" and "Stay" command. Give him the one whistle blast and make him remain seated for a full minute before sending him to fetch. Praise him, though, when he returns with the bird.

Should he break shot and reach the bird and retrieve it to you, do not attempt to punish him. Rebuking him for delivering a shot bird to hand would only confuse the dog, planting the seed that there might be something wrong or unpleasant about the act of fetching. Merely accept the bird without comment and, removing any loose feathers from his mouth, order him to resume hunting.

A few more such outings, during which you devote yourself fully   209 to handling the dog while your helper shoots only those birds properly flushed and hupped to, should produce consistently good results. This is not to say that your flushing dog will become unconditionally steady to wing and shot after three or four such sessions, but he certainly will know exactly what you expect. If you nip his transgressions in the bud—never shooting at birds he breaks on and catching him before he can get to the dead bird if he's unsteady to shot—it will only be a matter of time before he decides that conformance is a lot less trouble for him.

STOPPING AT COMMAND WHEN TRAILING GAME

The flushing dog should be trained to "Hup" on command when on a hot trail, in order to stay within shotgun range. Even though closing in fast on his quarry, the dog should be stoppable—at least for a brief interval—to enable his owner to shorten the gap and keep the potential target from flushing beyond effective killing range.

Admittedly, this is asking a lot, probably too much of a dog under two years of age. But it is something your flusher should be trained into after he's acquired some degree of understanding that he is hunting for the gun. Actually, it is simply an extension of the gunner's control and, if previous training has perfected the dog's obedience to the "Hup" command by voice, whistle, and upraised arm, obtaining the proper response should be possible even under the excitement of fresh, increasingly hot bird scent.

Since you don't want to stifle your dog's enthusiasm for hunting, there is little you can do if he refuses to halt while eagerly working a running bird. Use a loud whistle blast and a crisply voiced "Hup"

Above:
Giving your dog the directional command "Back," raise your arm overhead, leap forward, and swing your arm downward while simultaneously blowing two short blasts on your whistle. Photo by Robert Elman.
Below, left:
To send him right or left, call his name, raise your arm over your head, and command "Over" as you jump and swing your arm in the desired direction. Photo by Robert Elman.
Below, right:
Never fail to finish every training session in a friendly manner, lavishing praise and affection on your dog.

when he begins stretching the 35-yard limit. If he stops and sits obediently, waste no time in cautioning him to "Stay." Should he remain sitting until you reach him, tell him what a really great dog he is and release him quickly with the double-toot signal to go on.

By reinforcing your ability to "Hup" him on command when there are no birds present, you can train him to stop while he's busy zeroing in on a bird. Continue this aspect of his training and he'll eventually learn to let you catch up—part way, anyway. Only by having you reasonably close at hand when he flushes a bird will your dog ever get to retrieve it. When this fact sinks in, you can be pretty certain your dog will be more cooperative when it comes to waiting for you.

RETRIEVING BY HAND SIGNALS

Many upland bird hunters may not care to teach their flushing dogs to retrieve through the use of hand signals, at least not in the highly formalized manner employed by serious field trialers. That decision, of course, is a matter of personal preference. It may be argued that, since he is seldom used to hunt covey birds, the average flushing dog is not normally called upon to mark and retrieve multiple falls. Therefore, if he can't mark and successfully fetch a single downed bird, he might better be palmed off on someone who will appreciate a lovable house pet.

Still, acquainting your upland bird flusher with the fundamentals of following directional hand signals to locate a bird he may not have seen fall or may have marked poorly has practical value. After all, doubles on pheasants, grouse, or woodcock have been known to happen to a skillful, or lucky, scattergunner.

One of the first things you should do, when your dog is learning to become steady, is give him a line. This means pointing out a direction you are commanding your dog to follow to make a retrieve. He should run straight out on the course you have indicated with your left arm alongside his muzzle, until he sights or scents the dead bird or dummy, or is "Hupped" to receive further directional assistance.

To teach your dog to take a line, place him in the sitting position, order him to stay while you walk out about 75 feet and drop a dummy in an open spot where it is unmistakably visible. Going back to the dog, point to the dummy, then, as you pull your arm part way back and simulate an underhand tossing motion, command "Fetch" and release him with two toots on the whistle. He should experience no problems in making a few such retrieves, during which time he's beginning to learn to follow the line you indicate. Gradually increase the distance at which you plant the dummy to about 50 or 60 yards, always making sure your dog can see it plainly.

Soon you should drop the dummy in higher cover, out of sight of your dog, giving him a line but forcing him to hunt a bit for the retrieve. Once this phase is progressing well, the next step involves your secreting the dummy somewhere in the cover while your dog is still crated in the car. Take him out, sit him at your side, give him the proper line and send him to retrieve. It's likely he'll undercast on his first "blind" retrieve, so make sure you don't place the dummy—which should be sprinkled with a few drops of bird scent—too far away. The idea of the "blind" retrieve is to make your dog realize that whenever you give him a line, whether or not he's heard a shot or seen a bird dropped, there will be something for him to fetch.

When your dog is taking a line satisfactorily, you can start his instructions in fetching by hand signals. This is customarily taught by hupping your dog and telling him to stay while you let him observe you place a dummy about 75 feet immediately behind him or to his right or left. The dummy should be dropped in very close-cropped grass so as to be readily visible.

Walking back, take up a station about 35 feet directly in front of your dog. To teach him the most important and probably the most difficult of these signals—to turn around and cast directly behind him—start with the dummy so placed. Call his name to get his attention and raise your arm straight overhead. Command "Back" as you leap ahead and swing your arm downward, as though making a stiff-armed throw, and simultaneously giving two sharp blasts on your whistle.

Even though he has seen you place the dummy, he may be a bit confused over the new command and your sudden jumping antics. If so, just continue jumping in his direction and repeating the entire sequence—his name, "Back," the arm signal, and the double toot on the whistle. When he eventually fetches the dummy to you, pet and praise him generously.

Sending him either to the right or left involves the same basic routine. Call his name, raise your arm over your head, command "Over," while concurrently swinging your arm (your left or right, depending on which direction you want to send him) and jumping a step in that direction as you blow the two-blast whistle signal. Again, should he show confusion, keep repeating the whole sequence until he complies.

Once perseverance and repetition in these exercises have paid off,   213 and your dog clearly understands what you want when you order him "Back" or "Over," you should switch from a visible to a hidden dummy. With the same procedure and set of directional hand, voice, and whistle signals, you should have him gradually going farther to make his pickups and returns.

Eventually, you can combine his taking a line with these commands and halting him with the whistle blast while he's still a fair distance from the "blind" dummy. From his sitting position he'll rivet his attention on you, seeking directional help to locate the dummy. Utilize the breeze to the fullest extent as you direct him so he'll be able to employ his nose and not become too dependent on you to pinpoint every pickup.

With lots of time and patient tutelage, you can make your flushing dog a crackerjack performer, one that will hunt diligently, flushing his birds decisively and retrieving them eagerly and efficiently; in short, a well-mannered, highly polished individual whose work will please you and bring applause from anyone who hunts with the two of you. The best part of owning and hunting a flushing dog is the fact that, even with the minimum amount of training, you'll be able to enjoy a day afield and put some birds in your pocket, too. How far you want to take your flushing dog is something only you can decide.

CHAPTER 12

COMMON PROBLEMS AND THEIR SOLUTIONS

In training your bird dog, it is guaranteed that you are going to encounter some difficulties along the way. A few of these may be unique to your situation, but it's far more likely that the majority will be long-time problems that everyone who has ever been in a dog trainer's boots has had to face.

In many instances, such problems are created by the trainer's lack of experience and foresight in recognizing potential or embryonic-stage difficulties. Following closely, though, is plain, inexcusable carelessness about the need for observing consistency and regularity in training a bird dog. Only a few problems can be attributed to inherited flaws in a dog's physical and mental makeup.

This chapter will examine the most commonly experienced problems and will suggest solutions that have been effective for other owners and trainers. It is hoped you won't run into every predicament outlined, but familiarizing yourself with all of them may help you to avoid some. Also, not every solution offered will prove to be the correct one for you and your dog. As we've emphasized several times, every dog is an individual and is best handled as such.

Having established a close rapport with your dog, you should be able to "read" him fairly well. All those telltale signs he flashes unconsciously can help you anticipate actions and reactions. 215

Whenever you can, prevent him from making a mistake and perhaps avoid a potential problem.

Most of the difficulties examined here apply both to pointing and flushing dogs. Where the problems and their solutions pertain more to one type than the other, it will be so specified.

RANGING TOO FAR

A universal complaint of the neophyte bird dog trainer is that his dog ranges too far while hunting. Although not necessarily a fault in the pointing dog, it is an intolerable defect in the flushing dog, which must stick close enough to the gunner to provide him with an effective chance on flushed birds. Since the problem is more acute in the flushing dog, let's consider him first.

Normally, if the spaniel or retriever has been properly trained to quarter in the methodical manner previously described, he'll only quest beyond gun range for two reasons: to investigate a particularly birdy piece of cover; or when he's eagerly making game on a strong-running bird. If he continually ranges too far, you have probably slipped up earlier. There are several things you can do.

Initially, it's advisable to go back to that stage in his education where the bad habit originally was formed and approach his training as if it were brand new. Also, make certain he really knows what the whistle signal to turn means, and drill him in it for several days. If he indicates a disregard for your whistle order to turn, then you may have to take more drastic measures, such as snapping a 50- or 75-foot check cord on him and signaling him to turn just before he reaches the end of it. A sharp tug should convince him of what the whistle means.

In really hard cases, planting a few game birds strategically within the 30-yard left and right limits and working your flushing dog into them on the check cord will get the idea across to him that the majority of birds he seeks can be found closer to *you*. Killing several of these, and letting him retrieve them, should promote the connection after three or four outings.

The pointing dog that ranges too far can be both an annoyance and a hindrance. Noticed early enough, he can be encouraged to hunt closer by constant work in very dense cover while he's still young and impressionable. As with the flushing dog, he can also be taught more responsiveness to the whistle. The only trouble with this is the probable creation of a too mechanical hunting pattern, something undesirable and essentially uninteresting in a pointer.

216

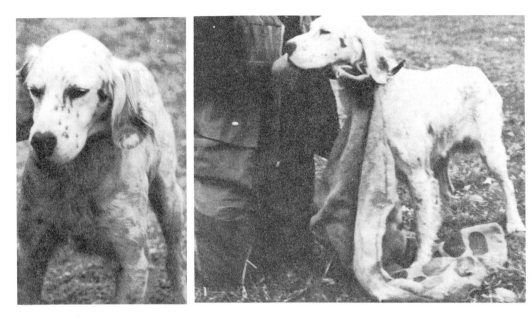

Left:
One artificial means of restricting a dog's range is affixing a length of heavy chain to his collar. The length and weight of the chain will depend on how much he needs to be restricted.
Right:
Attaching one corner of an empty 50-pound burlap sack to your dog's collar is another way to impede his range and speed.

Work on a long check cord can be effective, but often results in basically the same methodical quartering that can be accomplished by the whistle signal to turn. Commencing with a long check cord and, as response dictates, shortening and permitting your dog to drag it can make him more responsive to your voice or whistle commands to swing right or left without producing any overly artificial ground pattern.

As with the flushing dog that is inclined to push beyond reasonable range, the pointing dog can be lured into sticking closer by an abundance of birds. Three or four quail planted in a small field on a commercial shooting preserve provide ideal incentive. Check cording the dog into one of the first birds, while repeating the word "Clo-o-o-se," conditions him to a new command that means he'll find birds in proximity to his boss. Repetition generally proves successful.

217

Another method, totally artificial but sometimes the only recourse, is affixing some contrivance to the dog's collar that's designed to impede his progress. This can take the form of a 40-inch piece of garden hose or heavy chain that drags between his legs and limits his ability to run freely, or an empty 50-pound burlap sack, one corner of which is attached to his collar with the remainder allowed to drape in front, which appears like an oversize apron that he steps on with every three or four strides.

A variation of these range-restricters was described in my earlier book, *The Practical Hunter's Dog Book* (Winchester Press, 1971). The late Pert Prince, professional gun dog trainer and breeder and handler of numerous pointing dog field trial competitors nicknamed the device, "Bolos." Resembling the *bolloderos* of the famed gauchos of Argentina, the implement was made from two different lengths of light plastic cord suspended from a snap that was easily

---

Opposite:
Still a third range-trimming variation is a device nicknamed "Bolos," resembling the bolloderos of the Argentine cowboy.
Below:
A close up of the homemade "Bolos" reveals that blocks of wood can easily be substituted for solid rubber balls.

attached to any dog collar. Hanging from the end of each cord was a solid rubber ball, slightly less than 3 inches in diameter. The ball on the shorter cord barely reached the ground, but the one on the longer line dragged with about 6 inches to spare.

When the bolo was snapped to a dog's collar, the motion of his running would cause the weighted cords to swing freely and periodically twist one or the other of them around his front legs, thereby slowing him down, reducing his range and keeping him close enough to control.

Even though such factitious means can keep your dog in closer, it's almost inevitable that the moment you dispense with them, he'll

---

Opposite:
Hardmouth can sometimes be corrected by making your dog retrieve cold birds fresh from the refrigerator. Photo by Gary's Pets & People, courtesy of the American Brittany Club.
Below:
Bolting is a fault that definitely requires a reevaluation of your training techniques, which may be too harsh or too wishy-washy.

once again begin hunting at his natural range. For that reason it's far better to foresee a ranging problem early and try correcting it by more natural methods.

RANGING TOO CLOSE

Seldom a problem with the flushing breeds, ranging too close can be highly frustrating for the pointing dog owner. The versatile hunting breeds are more prone toward sticking too close to the gun than are the traditional pointers and setters, probably because of the tendency these dogs have of relying too much on ground trailing rather than on aerial or body scent.

If the problem stems mainly from a dog's predisposition to fiddle around, needlessly wasting time on old scent, your prospects of correcting the habit are usually good. Get on him whenever he starts

Facing and Below:
Deliberate bumping of birds necessitates a reinforcement of the meaning of the "Whoa" command, something that can be done daily at the feed pan or . . . in the field, by check cording your dog on planted birds.

to potter; tell him in no uncertain terms how unhappy you are with such foolishness and give him your beep-beep whistle signal to "Go On." A swat on the rump with your flushing whip may be necessary to get the idea across, but whatever you have to do, make sure you keep him moving out ahead.

Another way to get a plodder to reach out farther is to hunt him with a speedier, more rangy dog. The spirit of competition thus evoked sometimes can bring out a bit more range, if it's actually there. If it's not, however, there's really very little you can do; it's impossible to build range into a dog.

BLINKING

One of the most serious faults in an otherwise well-trained and seemingly perfectly mannered bird dog is the habit of "blinking" birds. This problem arises when the dog makes a conscious effort not to find birds.

How, you might wonder, can a bird dog reach the stage where he seeks to avoid, rather than find, birds? Almost without exception, the "blinker" is a man-made product, a victim of the owner who bears down too hard, usually when trying to steady his dog to wing and/or shot. Sometimes the cause can be traced to overly strict discipline in attempts to staunch a pointing dog on his birds. Whether he's a pointing or flushing dog, the reason he becomes a blinker generally can be pinpointed by a fear associated with the finding and handling of birds.

If you turn into an ogre every time your dog locates and begins working birds, constantly barking out admonitions, yelling at him to watch his step, whistling for him to "Hup" or "Whoa," and charging in like a bull elephant, and perhaps roughing him up for making a mistake, it's likely that he'll soon begin dreading the routine. Birds suddenly become a source of keen displeasure for him. Putting two and two together, your dog decides to steer clear of contacting birds and thereby preclude the unpleasantness their presence always brings. When he arrives at this stage, you will have your work cut out for you and no one but yourself to blame.

How will you know if your dog is becoming a blinker? One sure sign is his nervousness when he scents birds, something the beginning or amateur blinker exhibits noticeably. If you are walking up birds fairly consistently, which your dog's hunting pattern should have led him to point or flush, according to his type, you should begin to suspect the worst.

Give him every possible opportunity to prove your suspicions wrong. But if you have no reason to question his nose and he continues to pass up birds that you bump into, then you must be enough of a realist to recognize the problem. Your best solution is to relax your discipline to a bare minimum and give him as much gentle treatment and attention as possible, at home as well as afield. Forget most restraints, convince him that you're his pal, reestablish the kind of close companionable rapport that will allay his fear of reprimand.

Quit working and hunting him for a while and concentrate on really

Dropping on point is nearly always a man-made fault. It's serious and can often lead to even more serious problems such as blinking.

making friends with him again. When he evidences that he has regained his trust and respect for you, get him into some birds, but make no attempt to handle or instruct him. If he's a pointing breed, try making a wide circular approach to his point, coming in from the front to make the bird take flight over him. This should make him eager and excited. It also will take his attention off you. Should he decide to break and chase, let him. Whatever will help rekindle his verve in contacting birds should be encouraged to the hilt.

His zest for birds can be further increased if you kill a few over him and permit him to retrieve them, mouthing and even mauling several in the process. The key to curing the blinker is to rebuild his confidence in the fact that finding birds is fun and that they no longer result in harsh words, nagging reprimands, or punishment.

Like so many other problems, there are varying degrees of blinking. In the most extreme cases, it becomes necessary to retrogress, treating the dog like a five- to six-month-old pup and forsaking all semblance of discipline and control. The idea is to try to restimulate his basic hunting desire and urge to find birds to fever pitch once again.

Obviously, you must not attempt to hurry the cure. Only when your dog evidences a strong comeback interest in finding birds for you should you gradually begin reestablishing control according to the methods suitable for your type of dog. During the process, reexamine your own actions, making sure not to commit the same mistakes that caused your dog to become a blinker.

BOLTING

Unlike the blinker, the dog that bolts and runs away from his owner is seldom bird-shy; quite the contrary, as a rule. The "bolter" eagerly seeks his first opportunity to leave his owner and hunt for himself, fully cognizant that he can have a ball, doing just what pleases him—finding, busting, and chasing birds—with complete impunity.

Many of the dogs that bolt do so because they have been subjected to overly demanding discipline, rough punishment, and constant hacking by their owners. These dogs love bird hunting but, unfortunately, don't extend the same emotion to their owners. Generally, such dogs are of tough, bold temperament, something in their favor since unwise treatment wasn't able to destroy their natural bird-hunting instincts.

However, there are some bolters that acquire the habit strictly because of owners whose ineffectual handling and wishy-washy training demands have never really produced any proper respect for authority in their dogs. These dogs obviously need to be taught obedience with a firm and persevering hand. The best place to start is right at the beginning, going through the entire course of yard-training. If you recognize yourself as the owner of such a dog, you should certainly reevaluate your whole initial approach to his training, resolving to adopt a "take charge" attitude in instructing your dog. Naturally, that doesn't mean going to the other extreme, either.

After you've reestablished proper control of your dog in the yard, you'll have to transfer it to the field. A 50- to 75-foot check cord can be used to good advantage to keep him hunting close, where you can maintain better control and prevent his bolting at the first opportunity. Until you're convinced that he's learned his new lessons well, let him continue to drag a long check cord every time you work or hunt him.

If he bolts again after you dispense with the check cord, snap it right back on, let him know how displeased you are, and quit hunting him for the day. Repetition of this procedure should get through to him the fact that he either hunts with and for you, or he doesn't hunt at all.

If you have been overharsh with your dog, the same advice about reevaluating your training approach applies equally as well: your demands must be tempered, your rough hand softened, and your continual hacking suppressed. Even though your dog may be of bold disposition, you must stop hunting or working him for a while and make a determined effort to establish the kind of close rapport you should have achieved at the outset.

Relax and have some fun together, make him feel puppyish, take him with you wherever you go, as often as you can. And, above all, refrain from giving him too many orders. Your goal should be to replace the disdainful feeling your dog has had for you with a new respect born of affection rather than fear.

When you begin to see a definite change in his attitude, you should start taking him afield again. It's a good idea the first few times to take him to a commercial shooting preserve, where you can let him find plenty of birds under controlled circumstances. Work him on a check cord, just for added security, but remember to give him as few orders, signals, or admonitions as possible. Kill as many birds as you can afford and let your dog retrieve them, praising him effusively for a job well done.

Such tactics frequently will cure bolting in most dogs that have acquired the habit for the reasons cited. In the most unusual or severe cases, sometimes seen in field trial type pointers, you might have to resort to some means of artificial range-restricting device. In these extreme cases a length of chain—the weight of which is determined by how much stamina the dog possesses—attached to his collar or a special harness is often the only solution. In desperation, some owners use the electronic shock collar to convince the confirmed bolter that he's better off hunting for the gun. If nothing else works, there's no harm in trying the shock collar.

HARDMOUTH

Sooner or later, any dog trained to retrieve can be expected to deliver a bird to hand that appears somewhat mangled. The purist, quite predictably, yowls his displeasure at his dog's sudden acquisition of the intolerable fault of "hardmouth."

Yet, to a majority of upland gunners, a hardmouthed dog is one that consistently brings in birds that are literally unfit to bother dressing. Most upland bird hunters do not object to a few skin punctures in a retrieved bird, especially one that may only have been grassed. It stands to reason that a running cripple cannot be picked up as gingerly or carried as delicately as a bird that's stone dead.

However, if you observe your dog deliberately crunching down on his birds, crippled or otherwise, you can safely assume you have trouble. Since it isn't going to improve with time—in fact, once they start, hardmouth tendencies always get worse—the problem should be dealt with immediately.

Hardmouth is usually more easily corrected in a dog with bold temperament. The timid, nervous dog inevitably presents more of a challenge, since gruff tactics only worsen a bad situation.

Cures for hardmouth range from making your dog retrieve dummies festooned with sharp nails or birds containing hidden skewers to wrapping dead birds in hardware cloth. All of these methods are designed to encourage a tender carry. Some of them work on some dogs; some work on others not at all, the latter types quickly returning to their hardmouth ways in the field.

Probably the best method of curing it is to have your dog retrieve dead birds that have been thoroughly chilled in the refrigerator. They are stiff and, if your dog does start to crunch down, the cold flesh will bother his teeth. Letting him retrieve only refrigerated birds—maybe six retrieves at a clip—for a week or ten days should find him picking up and carrying a lot more gently.

Closely following the cold-bird treatment, switch him to fetching live birds fitted with spiked harnesses (described in Chapter 8). At first, make sure you tape the birds' feet and wings, thus preventing your dog from getting scratched or battered, something that usually encourages hardmouth. The spikes on the harness will ensure that your dog mouths the live bird very tenderly.

When he's performing satisfactorily, mix up the retrieves with cold and live birds in harness for a few more days. Then remove the tape from the feet of one of the live, harnessed birds so he'll be able to run, and give your dog some practice fetching "cripples." Soon, he should be able to safely retrieve wing-taped live birds, sans harness, and deliver them safe and sound.

Although the foregoing is suggested as a possible cure for hardmouth, it also provides an excellent training procedure for introducing the young flushing dog to retrieving birds and thereby encouraging tender pickup and carry.

GUNSHYNESS

If you've followed the procedures outlined in Chapter 6, gunshyness should be a problem you only read or hear about—unless you have allowed yourself the unaffordable luxury of carelessness while you or your companions afield were shooting around your dog. If for any reason your dog has become gunshy or even "gun tender," you have only two options: give the dog away as a house pet; or retain the services of a professional trainer whose specialty is curing gunshys. Some professional specialists guarantee results or they accept no payment.

You may wonder why we don't suggest a solution by which you can cure gunshyness. The reason is not a cop-out; it's merely that we don't believe the average bird dog owner is equipped psychologically to cope with the protracted nature of the cure. Part of the long, often frustrating method employed involves withdrawing the dog's food when he leaves his just-set-down feed pan at the sound of gunfire. Few owners who have established close bonds of affection with their dogs have the stomach or the necessary willpower for successfully completing the cure.

The best way to avoid the problem of gunshyness is to exercise moderate caution and common sense when you first introduce your pup to the gun, as well as in all later outings and hunts. However, if the ugly scourge should haunt your doorstep, don't hesitate to call upon professional help.

BUMPING BIRDS

Strictly a pointing dog problem, bumping birds—running into and flushing birds with no attempt to point—can make the offending dog look pretty ineffective, or just plain out fractious. But before you can do much about it, you'll have to try to determine whether he's bumping birds accidentally or knocking them on purpose.

Inadvertent bumps can be traced to a variety of reasons. Dry, dusty conditions or still green vegetation create scenting difficulties for any dog. Little or no breeze to carry scent often means a fast-moving dog can easily overrun his nose. And, sometimes, your dog's nose just may not be up to par; a cold or some other infection can impair his olfactory sensitivity. Thus, it's important that you determine as accurately as possible why he's bumping, before attempting any corrective action.

After a number of occasions, if you're sure your dog is bumping birds intentionally, give him the order to "Whoa" by voice and whistle. Go to him and, escorting him ungently back to the place where he knocked the bird, position him on point. Repeat "Whoa" very firmly four or five times as you make him stand stock still, then step out ahead of him and flail the brush with your flushing whip as if trying to flush a bird. Make certain your dog remains motionless all the while, cautioning him whenever necessary to "Whoa." When he's stood fast during your little act, which should take about two minutes, finally release him with the "All Right" whistle order.

Constant repetition of this is necessary to correct his knocking birds deliberately. Every time he bumps on purpose he must be chastized and set back up again on point. Under no circumstance should you ever shoot at a bird your dog has bumped deliberately. Some owners are content to shoot birds that their dogs put up accidentally, as long as the dogs immediately stop to flush. Personally, though, we suggest refraining from firing at any bird your dog doesn't point staunchly, at least during his first two or three seasons.

Besides the foregoing method of curing the problem, check cording your dog on planted birds often works well. If available, Coturnix quail are excellent birds for the purpose. They normally burrow right into the grass and lie very tight to a dog's point, encouraging staunchness. Let your dog work into the vicinity of the "plant" and, when he begins making game, caution him. Should he attempt to rush in and flush, simply restrain him with the check cord and command "Whoa." As soon as he begins pointing regularly, kill a few of the birds and let him retrieve them.

230

SOFTENING OR DROPPING ON POINT

Good, staunch, high-styled points are the hallmark of the class shooting dog. Of course, as some homespun country philosopher once observed, "Ya can't eat pointin' style." True, many of the productive "meat dogs" seen afield find and stand birds as staunchly as rocks, but with the posture of a sick calf. And at least part of the thrill of hunting birds with a pointing dog stems from the sight of an intense, stylish pointing stance.

While lack of pointing stylishness is not really a fault, softness and/or dropping on point are very definite problems. Softening manifests itself as a distinct relaxation of a dog's rigidity on point as the owner moves closer. The nearer the gunner approaches, the lower the dog sinks, his tail dropping and his overall stance appearing more flaccid. In severe cases, the dog virtually wilts and takes on the appearance of cringing in fright. Dropping on point is usually indicative of the worst stages of softening.

Generally, both faults are the result of an owner's excessively stern discipline in earlier training. Naturally, if the dog fears his owner, his apprehension exhibits itself most noticeably while he's pointing, since that act always brings his owner in close physical contact with him. At such times, the dog knows he's most accessible for punishment, a factor that can often lead him to associating birds with something unpleasant. And that will make him a prime candidate for becoming a blinker.

The solution for curing either of these very serious faults is the same treatment suggested for dealing with the blinker, the main difference being that unless softening has reached the extreme level, you don't have to stop hunting and working your dog. Just calm his apprehensiveness by curbing your strong disciplinary tactics. Talk to him as little as possible when you walk up to his points. If he breaks and goes with the bird, let him, but, of course, do not shoot at it. And, certainly, don't reprimand him.

Give him his head a bit, for a while, before gradually reintroducing milder discipline. Whenever possible, position him gently while he's on point, softly stroking him, elevating his tail, and encouraging confident intensity. Ultimately, you should begin talking reassuringly to him when you come to his points.

Not infrequently, dogs that point wild birds with style and intensity exhibit a softening and tail flagging (slight wagging or fluttering at the tip) when pointing planted birds. Lingering traces of human scent left on the birds tell the dog that this is a phony setup and, while he'll

231

go along with it to a degree, he simply won't point with the same fervency. This behavior should not be confused with the handler-induced problems of softening or dropping on point.

The dog that flags and sags a bit on planted birds can usually be tightened up by your acting more excited and making a bigger display of flushing the planted bird. Be careful, though, to make certain he doesn't begin moving forward or sideways off his original point rather than merely tightening up.

In coping with any of the common problems described, you must keep in mind that no two dogs ever are exactly the same, physically, or psychologically. The method that will solve a problem for someone else's dog may not even come close to curing the difficulty in yours. But the right prescription can usually be concocted by an analytical owner. Take the time to study and observe your dog carefully; familiarize yourself with his peculiarities; learn what makes him tick.

Don't be afraid to modify the foregoing solutions in any way you believe will make them more applicable to your dog. By using your imagination, you can dream up inventive variations to solve a specific problem. And sometimes just a small innovational change in a standard procedure will produce the desired results.

CHAPTER 13

A
PINCH
OF
SALT

In the previous chapter some of the most common problems the upland bird dog owner is apt to encounter while trying to train his dog to become a serviceable canine hunting partner were examined. This chapter will offer some observations on a few of the novice trainer's most frequently committed mistakes and common weaknesses. Some of these have already been enumerated, but there are others.

IMPATIENCE

Probably the most widespread and most calamitous error attributable to the neophyte trainer is trying to rush his bird dog's education. It's human nature to be impatient, to want to complete a job or project as quickly as possible, whether it's painting a house or building a patio. But pushing a young dog beyond his mental and/or physical capacities almost always results in either turning him into a timorous neurotic or a total automaton. Neither type will ever amount to much as a practical hunting field assistant that will help put very many birds in the game pocket.

Take your time in instructing your young dog, making certain he has thoroughly understood and retained one lesson before you push

233

on to another. And don't attempt to crowd too much into any single training session just because your dog may seem slow on the uptake. A couple of ten-minute periods are far better than one twenty-minute lesson. Remember that a puppy's attention span is extremely short and if you bore him with too much at one time, you'll lose ground rather than make progress.

INCONSISTENCY

Next to impatience, the most glaring deficiency in the new trainer is inconsistency. Disciplining a dog today and permitting him to get off scot free for the same offense tomorrow is a prime example of how not to obtain proper results.

Always be consistent in your commands and procedures while training, working, and hunting your dog. Never issue an order you are not ready to enforce. If you're not in a position to follow through and make your dog comply, then postpone giving him the command until you can see that it's carried out. If you condone slovenly or sluggish compliance, you can be certain that's exactly what your dog will give you.

Equally important, never try to fool your dog. For example, don't give him an order to "Fetch" if you know there's nothing for him to retrieve. In all training, success depends on trust and respect, and fooling your dog is no way to build those qualities.

LACK OF RAPPORT

Throughout this book we have tried to stress the importance of establishing close rapport with your bird dog. The close bond of friendship you form with your dog while he's a puppy will greatly influence the ease with which you'll be able to teach him all future lessons. Yet, many first-time bird dog owners neglect this aspect, believing that a few minutes of playing with their dogs every couple of days suffices.

Real companionship extends farther than that; it means showing genuine affection for your dog and sharing at least part of your relaxation time with him. It means letting him get involved with you, in lots of little ways—accompanying you to the store; going along on family picnics; tagging along on vacation; in short, practically any place he's not unwelcome.

Such continual close contact creates an unusually warm personal relationship and forges in the dog a strong desire to please and win

Left:
Impatience, the worst sin of all, can lead to pushing a dog's
education too fast, often by overly harsh means.
Right:
Neglecting the close bond of friendship that should be established
between a man and his dog will ultimately reflect in the dog's
training and performance.

the approval of his owner. Obviously, while not desirable to keep hacking your dog, you must insist upon quick obedience to any given command during the development of this association.

The stronger this rapport becomes, the more eager your dog will be to please you; and the sooner the realization sinks in that the best way he can please you is to comply with your commands, the quicker you will be able to elicit proper responses to whatever you teach him. Therefore, it's to your advantage to get close to your dog as early in the game as possible.

235

FIELD ERRORS

To the uninitiated, the way an owner comports himself in the field may seem unimportant, insofar as it affects his dog's training. Actually, it is very important. The way you approach a pointing dog, how you flush a bird, when to refrain from shooting—all these things have a profound effect on the development of your bird dog and the manner in which he reacts. For example, rushing up to a young dog on point, excitedly cautioning him to be careful and steady, then stepping right in front of him and flushing a bird and shooting practically over his head, is guaranteed to produce problems.

The proper way to approach a dog on point is to come in from the side, swinging a bit wide and coming into the dog's field of view far enough away so that he will not be startled. When you attempt to flush the bird, it should be flown with your body between it and your dog. This maneuver tends to discourage a young dog from breaking wing to chase. Should he break, you must not shoot at the bird, holding your fire to prevent his retrieving a prize he doesn't deserve.

OVERHANDLING

Some owners seem to be convinced that training a dog and having him under good control necessitates a great display of handling. Much verbal, whistle, and hand signaling connotes a trainer who can order his dog hither and yon, but seldom pays much concern to whether the dog is demonstrating anything besides mere mechanical conditioning to commands.

Certainly, the dog with more than a built-in response to machinelike obedience will soon begin to disregard the continual barrage of commands and directions and, if he has anything on the ball, will overcome his exuberant owner's constant flow of orders. If the dog becomes too dependent on directions from his owner, then his master had better have a superior nose and more inherent bird sense so he can always direct his dog into pay dirt.

It goes without saying that the dog that is truly well trained and responsive is the one requiring an absolute minimum of handling by voice, hand, or whistle signal.

Many novice owners unknowingly commit errors in the field that have profound influence on the development of a young bird dog. This gunner is about to shoot directly over the head of his pointing setter, an act that could lead to making the dog gunshy. Photo courtesy of Winchester News Bureau.

Left:
Punishment, in the proper dose to fit the offense, should be meted out when necessary.
Right:
Praise for good performance is just as important to the development of a good bird dog as punishment is for misdeeds. It is the dog's sole reward.

PUNISHMENT

Although much has been said about verbal chastisement and ungentle handling of the dog that misbehaves, punishment has not really been defined or dwelt upon. To a great many trainers, punishment of an adult dog means inflicting some form of physical pain in order to get a lesson across. Surely, just as praise for good performance is employed as a suitable reward, so too must punishment be utilized as a penalty for admonishing a dog for miscues.

Many owners are convinced that lack of stern action implies weakness. They seldom equate resolve with anything less than phys-

238

ical coercion. The fact is, even though there are times when the switch or flushing whip should be laid on, applying it too liberally can diminish its psychological effectiveness. The dog that routinely receives a beating for each and every mistake will either become inured to the pain or become a fearful, sullen, and most unhappy performer.

By itself, punishment is not the panacea of the successful trainer. Its peak effectiveness is attained only when it is employed often enough to come as a psychological shock to an errant dog. When administered at exactly the proper instant, in precise measure to fit the crime, physical roughness will certainly have more of a lasting psychological jolt on a dog of average temperament than will the temporary bodily discomfort it inflicts. The short-lived pain of a whipping is quickly forgotten, but its startling effects—and memory of the wrongdoing that precipitated it—lingers on.

The most appropriate punishment for your dog is something only you can determine, taking into consideration your dog's individual disposition. If he is timid and sensitive, a whack or two across his front legs or on his backside may be tantamount to a sound thrashing for a bold, hardheaded dog.

PRAISE

Equally important as the need to punish your dog for misdeeds is the idea of praising him for good performance. Like all of us, the bird dog appreciates a word of praise when he does his job well. Normally, a pat on the head and a few exultant words will prove sufficient to keep him happy and eager to please.

Although rewards of food are generally not recommended, there are occasions when a tidbit or two can advance your dog's progress. This is especially true of young pups whose attentiveness can be heightened considerably when a tasty reward provides the incentive for prompt compliance.

RELEASED BIRDS

In most large metropolitan areas today, finding much open land with an abundance of wild game birds is becoming increasingly difficult. Thus, training a bird dog on native game offers far more of a challenge than it did a quarter century ago. For this reason, planted or released birds, either on private lands or commercial shooting preserves, have assumed a significant role in the initial schooling of young bird dogs. In fact, were it not for the availability of such

239

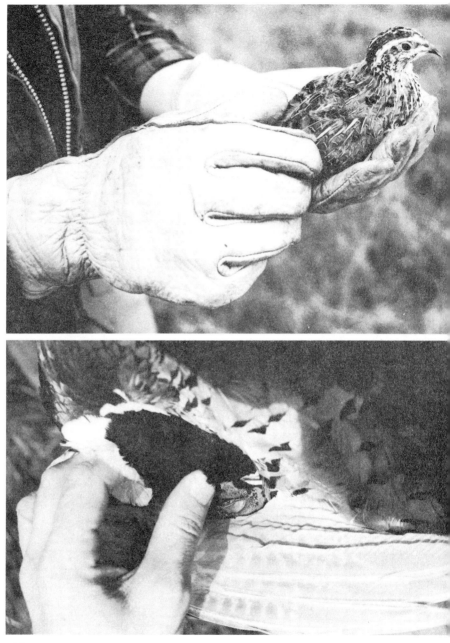

Above:
Many of today's bird dogs must be trained almost exclusively on released or planted birds such as this Coturnix quail.
Below:
Or this cock pheasant with its head tucked under its wing.
Opposite:
Or this bobwhite quail, most popular of all pen-raised game birds.

240

commercially raised game birds, many hunters in suburban regions might have to forsake bird dog ownership.

If you're more fortunate than many North American hunters and own or have access to a dozen or so acres of land, purchasing fifteen or twenty bobwhite quail that can be kept in a modest-sized holding or recall pen constitutes a genuine blessing. By releasing a few birds at a time—after a short conditioning period—you'll be able to work and train your dog just about at will.

There are a couple of approaches to keeping and releasing quail for so-called "backyard training" purposes. One involves using a recall pen as the bird's primary abode; the other utilizes a permanent holding pen and a small, easily portable recall trap. In either case, birds left in the recall pen or the recall trap will call the liberated birds back after you've

A small, easily portable recall trap is handy for taking afield. Two or three birds left in it will call back the quail that were liberated earlier for dog work.

This modest-sized holding pen easily accommodates up to 25 bobwhite quail without overcrowding. It can be built in just a few hours—or faster if you're very handy.

conducted your training session. The free quail are able to re—enter the pen or trap through conical, funnel-like openings similar in principle to the openings in a lobster trap.

Regardless of which system you choose, you'll need to build your own pen. Plans for a basic holding pen, which can be modified to serve as a recall pen, are included here. Our design safely accommodates up to a couple of dozen bobwhites without overcrowding. If you'd rather keep fewer birds, you can scale down the dimensions accordingly.

The materials you'll need include 2″ × 2″ and 2″ × 3″ lumber, 3/8″ and 1/2″ plywood, one-inch mesh poultry wire, 1/2″ mesh hardware cloth, some hinges and, of course, nails, staples and hooks-and-eyes.

243

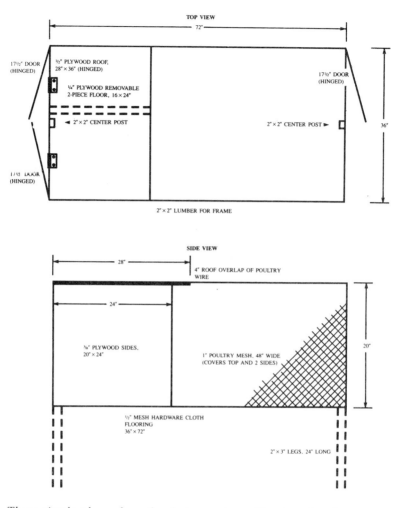

These simple plans show the design and specifications for the author's quail pen. As explained in the text, it can be built either as a simple holding pen or as a recall pen.

To modify the design from holding pen to recall pen will require adding two hardware—cloth funnel openings and deleting the $2'' \times 3''$ legs. In place of the legs will be four bricks, each laid flat under one of the pen's four corners. The conical funnel openings, one on each side, should be placed so that their centers will be no more than five or six inches higher than ground level when the pen is set on the bricks. This puts the openings head-high for a bobwhite and makes it simple for the birds to enter.

Half-inch mesh hardware cloth rolled into cone shape will serve as the re-entry ports. Tapering from about 5 inches at the mouth to approximately 3½ at the other end, the 7-inch-long cones must be angled up, with the small opening inside the pen a couple of inches higher than the birds' heads. To encourage quick and easy re-entry, the mouth of each cone should be mounted flush with the pen's side wire panel.

Whether you use the unit as a recall pen or simply as a holding pen will be a matter of personal choice. But, unless the dimensions of our design are scaled down by 25 percent or so, the pen will prove to be a bit cumbersome to lug to and from the field. For that reason alone you might opt for the permanent holding pen and then make or buy a handier-sized wire-mesh recall trap for use in field training. Several canine-supply catalog houses offer a reasonably priced call-back pen of easily portable dimensions ($8'' \times 16'' \times 30''$) that holds up to a dozen bobwhites.

The game-bird breeder from whom you buy your quail can provide you with all the needed information on their general care and feeding, so we'll skip that here. Be sure, though, to purchase birds-of-the-year. They will adapt readily to their new environment if they're no older than four or five months.

Before you attempt any dog work with your birds, they'll need a bit of conditioning to return to the recall pen. After being liberated several times and called back by their fenced-in buddies, the routine will become habit with all your birds. Colored plastic leg bands or a bit of colored yarn tied around a leg will help you keep track of which quail have been released and which ones need conditioning. Once the familiarization procedure has been completed, you can begin using the birds for dog training without undue fear of losing them.

Generally, within a couple of hours after each training session ends, the birds will all be back in the recall trap, ready to be returned to their regular holding pen.

Although there is obviously some effort and expense involved in keeping your own quail, it's basically a sweet system for providing your bird dog with the single most important reason for his being—birds.

Commercial hunting preserves, with their six-month open season, also offer excellent opportunities for dog training on live birds. Most preserves provide a choice of ring-necked pheasants, bobwhite quail, and chukar partridges. Some preserves offer programs specifically designed for training bird dogs, charging only a flat hourly fee plus an extra amount for any birds killed during your training session. The National Shooting Sports Foundation, Inc., 1075 Post Road, Riverside, Connecticut 06878, has a directory of commercial hunting preserves available free on written request.

Keeping some bobwhites of your own guarantees a ready and constant supply of birds for training purposes. With 15 or 20 quail always available, your gun dog will never lack opportunity to work on live game birds.

CONDITIONING YOUR DOG

Like most athletes, your bird dog must either be kept in tip-top shape or undergo a preseason conditioning program to fit him for the rigors of the public open hunting season. Proper exercise to trim excess poundage, toughen soft feet, tone flabby muscles, and build stamina and lung power is needed in appropriate dosages. Naturally, care must be taken not to overdo or try to accomplish too much too quickly.

A regular exercise program of running for ten or fifteen minutes daily should begin about six weeks prior to the hunting season. After two weeks you can gradually increase these exercise periods by

246

several minutes over the next week, building steadily by a few minutes every week thereafter until your dog can safely handle a half-hour run every day.

YARD-TRAINING REVIEW

Along with physically conditioning your dog in preparation for each new hunting season, you should plan to review his yard-training

---

Along with physically conditioning your dog in preparation for each new hunting season, you should give him a yard-training refresher course. Put him through all his basic commands.

lessons to keep him mentally sharp and obedient. This will prove especially important after a long summer layoff.

If you can devote about ten minutes a day to a general review of all his commands, he should be tuned up within a week or ten days. Work on hand and whistle signals with special attention to "Whoa" or "Hup," whichever is appropriate to his type of working style. Run him through a couple of minutes of retrieving feathered dummies and, if possible, a pigeon or quail. Then when opening day rolls around, you'll be ready to go afield with a dog that is physically and psychologically conditioned to begin his job with proper enthusiasm.

Be sure to brush up on his retrieving practice by tossing a few dummies for him. Photo by Jerome Knap, courtesy of Jim Irwin.

A FINAL THOUGHT

No matter how far you've taken your dog along the road toward being a fully finished bird dog, you will have invested a fairly size-able chunk of time and effort. Of course, it's to be hoped that your investment pays off in solid dividends of pleasure-filled days marked by crisp autumn weather, colorful foliage, and an abundance of fast-flying upland birds.

Yet, simply because you have trained your dog to turn in the kind of performance that satisfies you now, don't lose sight of the fact that you cannot rest on your laurels. Keeping a good bird dog trained is a lifetime endeavor. But like the best cheese, a fine bird dog kept under the proper conditions improves with age.

CHAPTER 14

SOME
EXTRA
HELP

Let's not kid ourselves, neither you the reader nor I. There a bound to be times when, despite your best efforts, your dog's training bogs down. This book, or any other one for that matter, has its limitations; it cannot, for example, say: "Hey, pal, no wonder your dog isn't reliably staunch. Your approach when he's on point is too. . . ."

Flesh-and-blood observations—the human element—must be provided in certain situations to overcome some small "glitch," to offer a pearl of incisive wisdom, to demonstrate a particular technique or nuance of it. There is, in short, no possible substitute for individual, personal counsel and discussion in solving some training problems. But aside from seeking the services of a professional, where can you turn up some really worthwhile help, especially if you don't know anybody with gun dog training experience?

Although dozens of organizations are dedicated to dogs in general and/ or to gun dogs specifically, most of them are not in a position to offer training assistance directly. A majority, however, can and do offer some sort of information service that may send the gun dog owner in the right direction to find more tangible help.

Chief among these are breed clubs, the official sponsors and representatives of the purebred dogs eligible for registration in the American Kennel Club. Each breed has its own club, a national organization that supports and promotes it. The club secretary, whose name and address

251

can be obtained from the A.K.C., 51 Madison Avenue, New York, New York 10010, is responsible for answering correspondence and providing information relative to that breed and its sponsored activities nationwide. Although dog shows and obedience competitions generally head the list of such activities, field trials are also included in the case of the sporting breeds.

A letter of inquiry to the secretary of the club promoting your breed of gun dog can get you information on future field trials scheduled in your locality, state or region, including the names, addresses and phone numbers of the sponsoring organizations and their officials. Planning to attend one of these field trials certainly is a step in the right direction toward expanding your overall education in the world of bird dogs. Definitely a rewarding experience in itself, watching a field trial should provide you with valuable insights into how your breed is expected to perform in the field.

At a field trial, not only will you witness members of your own chosen breed at work, but you will also see others of different breeds, and this can give you a better perspective of bird dog performance in general. After watching a few braces, don't be surprised to find yourself mentally noting differences in dog' style and application, and starting to do your own evaluating of individual performances.

But just as important, attending a trial or two should enable you to meet and rub elbows with people who share a common, often a dedicated, interest in bird dogs, hunting and shooting. And, as you already know—or will soon discover—such folks are seldom reticent about their favorite subjects. Usually, all you have to do is ask a question or request an opinion, and their exuberance may have you listening for quite a while.

Listen attentively and you're sure to pick up a lot of good information plus some first-rate practical advice on gun dog training—which is really why you're there, after all. You can make any number of contacts at a field trial just by being a good listener. And, if you're really fortunate, you may form a worthwhile friendship or two and maybe end up getting some personal help in training your gun dog.

Aside from A.K.C breed clubs, of course, information on field trials is obtainable from other sources. Most of the pointing dog trials, for instance, are conducted by member clubs of the Amateur Field Trial Clubs of America, Inc. These member club trials are held in accordance with *The American Field's* "Minimum Requirements" rules and judgement standards, with recognized wins being recorded in the *Field Dog Stud Book*, the official registry maintained by The American Field Publishing Company.

Information on member field trial clubs in your area, state, or region is available by writing and enclosing a self-addressed stamped envelope with your request to: Ms. Linda Hunt, Secretary/Treasurer, Amateur Field Trial Clubs of America, Inc. (AFTCA), Danceyville, TN 38069.

Supplementing the AFTCA field trial clubs are several associations devoted to furthering interest in bird dogs and upland bird hunting through competitive field trials. Among them are The National Shoot-to-Retrieve Association (NSTRA), the National Bird Hunters Association (NBHA) and the American Bird Hunters Association (ABHA). Although each is a separate and distinct organization, they all share similar objec-

Training clinics are a specialty of the North American Versatile Hunting Dog Association. Here, NAVHDA trainer John O'Brien uses a training table to teach the "Whoa" command to his German short-haired pointer, Ridgerunner's Outlaw Jake. Photo courtesy of John O'Brien, NAVHDA.

Tips on training are openly shared by NAVHDA members, whose main goal is to help hunters develop efficient and versatile gun dogs. Here, judges and apprentices confer before beginning a Natural Ability test of Elena, a German wirehaired pointer owned by Dale Lyddon. Photo courtesy of Barb Jensen, NAVHDA.

Retrieving a duck at an Invitational Utility Test conducted by NAVHDA, wirehaired pointing griffon Sunny Branches Beau Brokk exemplifies the organization's goal of practical versatility. Photo
254   *courtesy of Barb Jensen, NAVHDA.*

Sight pointing a live pigeon tethered to a fishing rod is a technique demonstrated by NAVHDA trainer Paul Grefath and Gretchen, a German wirehaired pointer owned by Scott Mundrick. Photo courtesy of John O'Brien, NAVHDA.

---

tives: essentially to promote the fun and enjoyment of field trialing with the walking shooting dog and to stress the pointing dog's retrieving abilities.

Details on these organizations, their affiliated clubs' locations and trial schedules can be obtained by contacting the following individuals and including a stamped, self-addressed envelope with your letter:

John Everett, President, National Bird Hunters Association, 2900 McElveen Drive, Dalzell, SC 29040

Wes Barr, President NSTRA, 226 North Mill Street #2, Plainfield, IN 46168

Earl Elkins, President, American Bird Hunters Association, 701 Grove Road, Gatesville, TX 7652

Invaluable as all of the foregoing clubs and associations—and attendance of their field trials—can be, none of them is set up specifically to offer   255

Retrieving is fundamental to the practical gun dog, and NAVHDA training stresses its importance. Trainer John O'Brien is shown here as he receives a duck delivered tenderly to hand by his German shorthaired pointer, UT Happy Ridge Heidi of Marion. Photo courtesy of John O'Brien, NAVHDA.

owners direct help in training their gun dogs. However, such an organization does exist. The North American Versatile Hunting Dog Association, better known as NAVHDA, prides itself on "teaching you how to train your hunting dog."

Originally founded to support the continuing development in the U.S. and Canada of the so-called "Continental" or "versatile" pointing breeds, NAVHDA today opens its ranks to any and all pointing breeds and their owners. Extending its helping hand to new and inexperienced gun dog owners, the group's local chapters hold periodic training clinics where training methods and techniques of proven merit are patiently demonstrated by veteran NAVHDA members.

Unlike some professional gun dog trainers, NAVHDA members have no closely guarded trade secrets, but, rather, they prefer to share their knowledge and experience openly with those attending a training clinic. It's their avowed aim to try to help the hunter mold his pointing dog into an efficient, versatile gun dog, and the training clinic experts give unstintingly of their time toward that end.

As its very name implies, of course, development of versatility in the pointing dog is NAVHDA's primary goal. By definition, this means a dog that's as much at home in the duck blind as in the woods; that not only points game (furred as well as feathered) but retrieves it as well, both on land and in water.

Naturally, the NAVHDA training system stresses the dog's utility in the field. The stylish performance of the specialist, while appreciated by the group's members, is strictly secondary to the gun dog's practical function: to find and point game, then make sure it gets into the bag, by tracking it when necessary and/or locating it through the hand, voice and whistle signals of the gunner.

In addition to running training clinics, local chapters also conduct tests for young and finished dogs. For the pups, Natural Ability Tests, and for the polished veterans, Utility Tests challenge each to qualify, not against other canine competitors as in most field trials, but against a standard, with specific point values assigned to each phase.

Thus, NAVHDA may well prove to be your best source of extra help in getting through any rough spots in your training progress. Detailed information on NAVHDA membership, local chapters and training clinic schedules is available by writing to John F. O'Brien, 4302 Route 21, Marion, New York 14505. Please don't forget to include a stamped, self-addressed envelope with your letter.

APPENDIX

SUGGESTED READING

No single book on bird dogs and the various methods of training them can say it all—at least, we've never seen one. But where one book may lack sufficient detail on some aspects, another may shine. Then, too, books devoted to a specific type and breed of bird dog obviously can treat their subjects in a more detailed manner.

Although our advice to the person training his first bird dog would be to stick with one manual, to avoid confusion arising from differing philosophies, he'll profit from reading what other authors have to say about his particular type and breed of dog. Such additional material often can provide a new approach to an old idea that will stimulate the reader into using his own inventive talents to deal with a specific training problem.

Each of the books listed below offers considerable material of interest and potential benefit to the reader:

Pointing Dogs:

Bailey, J. *How to Help Gun Dogs Train Themselves.* Hillsboro, Oregon: Swan Valley Press, 1991.

Brenneman, Al. *Al Brenneman Trains Bird Dogs.* Huntsville, Alabama: Strode Publications, 1983.

Davis, H. P. *Training Your Own Bird Dog.* New York: Putnam, 1948.

Evans, G. B. *Troubles With Bird Dogs.* Piscataway, New Jersey: Winchester Press, 1975.

Falk, J. R. *The Practical Hunter's Dog Book.* Stillwater, Minnesota: Voyageur Press, Revised Edition, 1991.

Long, Paul. *All The Answers To All Your Questions about Training Pointing Dogs.* Slingerlands, New York: Capitol Bird Dog Enterprises, 1974

Robinson, J.B. *Hunt Close.* New York: Winchester Press, 1978.

259

Roebuck, K.C., *Gun Dog Training: Pointing Dogs*. Harrisburg, Pennsylvania Stackpole, 1983.

Wehle, R. G. *Wing & Shot*. New York: Country Press, 1964.

West, R. *Basic Gun Dog Training*. Des Moines, Iowa: Stover Publishing Co., 1993.

Winterhelt, S., and E. D. Bailey. *The Training and Care off the Versatile Hunting Dog*. Ontario: North American Versatile Hunting Dog Association, 1973.

Flushing Dogs:

Goodall, C. S. & Gasow, J. *The New English Springer Spaniel*. New York, NY: Howell Book House, 1984.

Irving, Joe, *Training Spaniels*. North Pomfret, Vermont: David A. Charles, 1980

Pfaffenberger, C. J. *Training Your Spaniel*. New York: Howell Book House, 1963 [new edition].

Radcliffe, T. *Spaniels for Sport*. New York: Howell Book House, 1969.

Roebuck, K.C. *Gun Dog Training: Spaniels And Retrievers*. Harrisburg, Pennsylvania: Stackpole, 1982.

Spencer, J. B. *HUP! Training Flushing Spaniels the American Way*. New York, NY: Howell Book House, 1992.

Retrievers:

Brown, W. F. *Retriever Gun Dogs*. New York: A. S. Barnes, 1945.

Fischer, G. *The Complete Golden Retriever*. New York: Howell Book House, 1974.

Free, J. L. *Training Your Retriever*. New York: Coward McCann, 1968.

Morgan, C. *Charles Morgan on Retrievers*. New York: Abercrombie & Fitch, 1968.

Quinn, T., *The Working Retrievers*. New York: E.P. Dutton, 1983.

Tudor, J. *The Golden Retriever*. London: Popular Dogs, 1966.

Wolters, R.A., *Game Dog*. New York: E.P. Dutton, 1984.

Wolters, R. A. *Water Dog*. New York: E. P. Dutton, 1964.

General and More Than One Type of Gun Dog:

Duffey, D. M. *Hunting Dog Know-How*. Piscataway, New Jersey: Winchester Press, Revised Edition, 1983.

Duffey, D.M., *Expert Advice on Gun Dog Training*. Piscataway, New Jersey: Winchester Press, Revised Edition, 1985.

Fergus, C. *Gun Dog Breeds, A Guide.* New York, NY: Lyons & Burford, Publishers, 1993.

Leedham, C. *Care of the Dog.* New York: Charles Scribner's Sons, 1961.

Moffit, E. B. *Elias Vail Trains Gun Dogs.* New York: Howell Book House, 1964 [new edition].

Vine, L. L. *Your Dog. His Health and Happiness.* New York: Winchester Press, Revised Edition, 1975.

BOOKLETS AND PAMPHLETS ON GENERAL CARE, FEEDING, TRAINING, ETC.:

Hundreds of booklets, pamphlets, and bulletins have been produced by the major U.S. manufacturers of dog foods and pet supplies on a wide variety of topics of importance to new or prospective dog owners. Many of these publications are available free or at nominal cost on written request. When writing to any of the companies listed below for a list of the publications they have available, it is suggested that your request be accompanied by a self-addressed, stamped envelope.

Agway, Inc., 333 Butternut Dr., DeWitt, NY 13214.

Alpo Petfoods, Inc., Rt. 309 & Pope Rd., Allentown, PA 18104.

Bench & Field, P.O. Box 46, New Paris, IN 46553.

Best Feed & Farm Supplies, Inc., 100 Union Ave., Oakdale, PA 15071.

Hartz Mountain Corp., 600 S. 4th St., Harrison, NJ 07029.

Iams Co., 7250 Poe Ave., Dayton, OH 45414.

Kal Kan Foods, Inc., 3250 E. 44th St., Los Angeles, CA 90058.

Quaker Professional Services, 585 Hawthorne Ct., Galesburg, IL 61401.

Ralston Purina Co., Inc., Checkerboard Square, St. Louis, MO 63164.

BIRD DOG PUBLICATIONS:

The American Brittany, 4124 Birchman, Fort Worth, Texas 76107.

The American Field, 542 South Dearborn Street, Chicago, Illinois, 60605.

The American Water Spaniel Club, 18515 Lake George Boulevard NW, Anoka, Minnesota 55303.

The German Shorthaired Pointer, Box 395, Saint Paris, Ohio 43072.

Gun Dog Magazine, P.O. Box 35098, Des Moines, Iowa 50315.

Gun Dog Supreme, Richard Bovard, ed., 2820 Edgewood Drive N., Fargo, North Dakota, 58102.

Retriever Field Trial News, 1836 E. Saint Francis Avenue, Milwaukee, Wisconsin 53207.

Spaniels in the Field, 10714 Escondido Drive, Cincinnati, Ohio 45249.

The Weimaraner, P.O. Box 351, LaCrosse, Wisconsin.

BREED REGISTRIES:

American Kennel Club, 51 Madison Avenue, New York, New York 10038. Registers all recognized purebreds.

The Field Dog Stud Book, American Field Publishing Company, 542 South Dearborn Street, Chicago, Illinois 60605.

The United Kennel Club, Kalamazoo, Michigan. Registers all breeds.

BIRD DOG TRAINING EQUIPMENT, SPECIALTY ITEMS, AND ACCESSORIES:

Sources of supply of various training equipment, canine specialty items, and other accessories are highly important to the bird dog owner. Most of those in the following listing have personally served our needs quite satisfactorily over the years:

General:

Dogs Unlimited, Box 1844, Chillicothe, Ohio 45601

Drs. Foster & Smith Inc., 509 Shepard Street, P.O. Box 100, Rhinelander, Wisconsin 54501

Dunn's Supply Store, Grand Junction, Tennessee 38039

E-Z Bird Dog Training Equipment Company, Box 333-A, Morganfield, Kentucky 42437

Gun Dog Supply, Box 320, 116 East State Street, Ridgeland, Mississippi 39157

Hallmark Supplies, Main Street, Menomonee Falls, Wisconsin 53051

Happy Jack, Box 475, Snow Hill North Carolina, 28580

Hulme Sporting Goods and Manufacturing Company, Box 670, Paris, Tennessee 38242

Kipewa Supplies, Box 15, Manotick, Ontario K4M 1A2, Canada

Nite Lite Company, Box 1, Clarksville, Arkansas 72830

Scott's Dog Supply, 9252 Crawfordsville Road, Indianapolis, Indiana 46234

Sporting Dog Specialties, Inc., Box 68, Spencerport, New York 14559

Tidewater Specialties, U.S. Route 50, Box 150, Wye Mills, Maryland 21679

Dog Crates and Station Wagon Barriers:

K. D. Kennel Products, 1741 North Broadway, Wichita, Kansas 67214
Kennel-Aire Manufacturing Company, 6651 Highway 7, St. Louis Park, Minnesota 55426

Kennel Fencing and Panels:

Bob Long Kennel Runs, Route 3 North, Gambrills, Maryland 21054
Brinkman Manufacturing and Fence Company, Route 8, Huntoon and Auburn Road, Topeka, Kansas 66615
Crest Kennel Company, 1900 West Bates Avenue, Englewood, Colorado 80110
Econ-o-Kennel, 6400 East 35th Street, Kansas City, Missouri 64129
Mason Fence Company, Box 711B, Leesburg, Ohio 45135

Doghouses:

Canine Pal Sales Company, 421 East 39th Avenue, Gary, Indiana 46409
Dogaloo Company, 6817 North 22nd Place, Phoenix, Arizona 85016

Index